After the riots
THE POLICE IN EUROPE

WITHDRAWN

After the Riots
THE POLICE IN EUROPE

Norman Fowler

DAVIS-POYNTER

LONDON

First published in 1979 by
Davis–Poynter Limited
20 Garrick Street WC2E 9BJ

Copyright © 1979 by Norman Fowler

ISBN 0 7067 0101 1

Printed in Great Britain by
Bristol Typesetting Co. Ltd, Bristol

To my Mother and Father

Contents

Acknowledgements

I would like to express my thanks to all those whom I interviewed during visits to:

WEST GERMANY
The Bavarian State Police
The Munich Police (now amalgamated)
The Bremen Police
The Hamburg Police
The *Bundeskriminalamt* in Wiesbaden
The Ministry of the Interior in Bonn
The Ministry of Justice in Bonn
The *Gewerkschaft der Polizei* in Hilden
Inter-Nationes

FRANCE
The National Police
The *Gendarmerie Nationale*
The Prefect of Police in Paris
The Ministry of the Interior
The Ministry of Defence
Interpol in Paris
The Council of Europe at Strasbourg

THE NETHERLANDS
The State Police
The Amsterdam Police
The Rotterdam Police
The Ministry of Justice in The Hague
The *Nederlandse Politie Bond* in Amsterdam
Foreign Workers Foundation in Rotterdam

ITALY
The Ministry of the Interior
The *Guardia di Pubblica Sicurezza*
Criminalpol in Rome
The Rome Police

A*

DENMARK
The National Police
The Ministry of the Interior
The Copenhagen Police

In addition my thanks are due to the police in Belgium, Luxembourg and Eire – while in Belgium, France and Italy I paid visits to companies of Securitas International. In the United States I would like to offer thanks to the New York traffic court administration and to the Los Angeles Police Department.

In Britain I would like to acknowledge the invaluable help given over a long period by many forces (most of all the Metropolitan Police for this work) the Police Federation, the Home Office and the Foreign Office.

Individual thanks are particularly due to Sir Robert Mark, Sir Leon Radzinowicz, Sir Alan Bullock, Philip Stead, Professor Alfred Heijder, Alec Mud, Reinhard Rupprecht, Karl Meyer, John Ling and the late Oliver Woods (who first asked me to write a series of articles on the police), and to the staff of the House of Commons Library.

Most of all my thanks are due to all the policemen who over the last four years have withstood my questioning and co-operated to make this book possible.

N.F.

Preface

In 1968 Europe was aflame with violent protest. Students battled with police in the streets of Paris; and in Berlin the riots which followed the attempted assassination of Rudi Dutschke prompted comparison with the last days of the Weimar Republic. In London, however, there was neither tear-gas nor water cannon. In spite of predictions that a major Vietnam war demonstration would lead to something close to armed insurrection the Home Office kept its nerve. Demands that it should be banned were resisted on grounds of principle that a traditional right to peaceful demonstration is recognized in Britain; and on grounds of practice that the prohibition of a demonstration usually makes the police job not easier but infinitely more difficult. It is the police who have to ensure that no demonstrators succeed in getting onto the streets. The October demonstration was seen as a vindication of the British way of handling these matters. Policemen marched side by side with demonstrators and, although there were casualties in Grosvenor Square, the toll was small in comparison with other major capital cities.

In Britain the result was welcomed by both public and police. To the public the demonstration seemed to show that – however unsuccessful we were in running our economy – there was still one area where Britain was held up as an example. We had a police force which was admired throughout the world. To the police (and to the authorities generally) the demonstration appeared to establish that even in protest the British public largely applied its own discipline and avoided violence. Other European countries reacted very differently. Governments were concerned at how near the riots had brought them to total chaos: the public was concerned at the violence and the often clumsy reaction of the authorities. The reputation of the police (the representatives of the authorities) hardly could have been lower.

1968 was a watershed. The importance of securing good relations between police and public was recognized as a prime aim of policy by virtually every government in the Common Market. This book seeks to examine the progress that has been made since then and the factors which influence such relations. It is not intended to be a slavish comparison of every aspect of police work nation by nation: that would be more appropriate for a technical manual. The aim is to see how different countries deal with the major issues of police policy today and to examine what lessons can be learnt. The hope is that the book will be read not only by policemen and those with a special interest in this area but by others who are concerned with the role of the police in a democratic community.

1

The Police Idea

Whether or not the British police is the best in Europe, it is certainly not the oldest. France had its first Lieutenant of Police in 1667, while the police system itself dates back to the thirteenth century; Berlin formed a state force in 1742; and the success of the police in Holland and Flanders was being held out as an example to the English as early as 1795. England, on the other hand, did not form its first professional force until 1829, and it was not until almost thirty years later that there was a truly national system. At the beginning of the eighteenth century, the very word 'police' was virtually unknown in England; a position which led one French visitor to complain: 'How can one expect order among these people who have not such a word as police in their language?' Even as late as 1763 a letter writer to the *Public Advertiser* claimed that he heard the word used for the first time in 'polite company'.

Gradually, however, the word did come into use and, as it did, it took on a definite and menacing meaning. Police meant the police of France. It conjured up an image of repression and it was seen as a direct challenge to the liberty Englishmen held so dear. In choosing between order and freedom, the English chose freedom and for almost one hundred years refused to believe that any balance could be struck between the two. They watched as crime and lawlessness rose, but their characteristic response was to give to the courts ever greater powers of punishment.

At the beginning of the nineteenth century the law reformer, Sir Samuel Romilly, remarked that there was 'probably no other country in the world in which so many and so great a variety of human actions are punishable with the loss of life as in England'. During George II's reign, thirty-three new capital offences were created, and during the reign of George III a further sixty-three. In apparent contradiction, the criminal law procedure was remarkably liberal for the time, and French visitors enviously compared England's public trials by jury with their own inquisitorial process. But the English logic was that, as the rights of the accused were safeguarded, the punishment of those found guilty should be exemplary.[1]

The death penalty could be awarded for any offence, from murder of the King to marking the edges of coins, from riotous assembly to cutting hop binds; and from wounding to pick-pocketing. It was scarcely limited by age, and children over fourteen could be executed — and even some younger ones than that were hanged. Executions themselves were deliberately staged in public on the grounds that the more who saw them the greater would be the warning but the main effect seems to have been felt by employers who complained of high absenteeism on 'hanging days'. It seems strange that people who put so much faith in deterrents did not recognise earlier the deterrence of detection. But any proposal to form a professional police to tackle the rising number of criminals who were clearly unmoved by judicial threat was resisted as unconstitutional. To many the conclusive argument against such a police was the French example.

Under Louis XIV's edict of 1667 a Lieutenant of Police (the title was later changed to Lieutenant General) had been appointed to take responsibility for the general security of Paris. But this was not his only duty. He was also responsible for dealing with its floods and fires; for inspecting its markets, inns and lodging houses; for ensuring an adequate supply of food; for checking weights and measures; and for controlling the press and, in particular, preventing the printing and distribution of protestant pamphlets. Thus right from the start the area of operation of the French police was remarkably wide; a fact which led Dr Johnson, when recognising the French origin of the word in his dictionary, to define police as 'the regulation and government of a city or country so far as regards the inhabitants.'

Yet what most foreigners (together with a great number of Frenchmen) found most objectionable about the French system of police was the employment of an army of spies, together with the general exercise of arbitrary power. The first lieutenant of police, Gabriel-Nicholas de la Reynie, had employed informers (*mouchards*) but it was his successor, the Marquis d'Argenson, who really established them as an instrument for prising out private information. Under d'Argenson, daily reports were presented to the King at Versailles and such reports continued throughout the years of the *ancien régime*. There were two bulletins: the *bulletin politique ou d'espionnage*, which covered such areas as the current state of public opinion; and the *bulletin moral*, which collated information on the sexual, drinking and gambling habits of the aristocracy, the clergy and the professions. It was nice irony that it was the system he had done so much to create which eventually revealed d'Argenson himself as a man who would have 'no mistresses other than nuns'.

As the eighteenth century progressed, surveillance was extended to such a degree that one head of police could boast that whenever there were three people talking in the street at least one of them was bound to belong to him. Informers were paid on a piece rate basis according to the information they provided, and recruits were plentiful. D'Argenson claimed that he drew most of his informers from amongst dukes and their lackeys, and one of the last of the Lieutenant Generals, Lenoir, considered physicians and surgeons invaluable as they could enter any house and 'receive confidences which they are ready to communicate.' On this intelligence base were built further refinements like the police section charged with intercepting the mail.

Inevitably such a system bred corruption. The police was subject to no external check, while the demands of ever more extensive surveillance meant that the police needed the co-operation of the very people they were there to control. Any use of informers must involve compromise but here compromise verged on the total as police allied themselves with the underworld. Thus as brothels could play a valuable part in collecting information, they were allowed on condition that the brothel keepers and the prostitutes returned daily lists of their clients, together with a list of their tastes. (One report reveals the not surprising fact that a Paris procuress was becoming worried about supplying girls for the Marquis de Sade). To complete this murky picture, the very finances of the police relied heavily on a tax on gaming and bribery so widespread that men grew rich in the service—including one *inspecteur* paid no more than four thousand livres a year who retired a millionaire.

By eighteenth-century standards, the forces at the disposal of the

Lieutenant General were immense. Paris was divided into twenty different divisions, headed by *commissaires de police,* and in each an *inspecteur* was responsible for both the professional detective work and the deployment of the informers. Civil order was maintained by well disciplined detachments of mounted and foot watch guards, who patrolled day and night; by sentries strategically placed throughout the city; and by patrol groups like the *archers,* whose origin went back long before 1667. These forces were amply armed but in case of emergency the Lieutenant General could always call on the military. Indeed, by the last years of the *ancien régime* army detachments were permanently stationed in likely trouble spots. Outside Paris law and order was in the none too tender hands of the *maréchaussée,* who had originally been formed to control soldiers on their way to camps and garrisons but whose role had been extended to civil crime in provincial France.

The strength of the French police lay not only in their numbers but also in their legal powers. Both the Lieutenant General and the *commissaires* could sit in a judicial capacity and try breaches of their own regulations; while the *maréchaussée* were empowered to try the offenders they themselves had caught—and for whose arrest they could receive a reward. The police also possessed extensive powers to enter homes day or night and arbitrary powers of arrest and interrogation. But unquestionably the most hated power of all, which gave France the final stamp of a police state, was the *lettre de cachet.* There were four classes of *lettres de cachet* but all had the same effect of detention without trial. Of the four classes it was the *lettre de cachet* concerning *affaires de police* which was the most used.

On the credit side it must be conceded that the French police kept order and that it was safer to walk in the streets of Paris than in virtually any other European capital. Certainly London could make no boast of safety and as Horace Walpole complained in 1752 'one is forced to travel even at noon as if one was going to battle.' Compared with France, the arrangements for preserving order and detecting crime in England were ramshackle and ineffective. The best ordered part of London was the City, which relied mainly on ill paid night watchmen who in the words of one police historian were mostly 'contemptible, dissolute and drunken buffoons, who shuffled along the darkened streets after sunset with their long staves and dim lanterns calling out the time and the state of the weather.'² Outside London, the traditional parish constable system was rapidly breaking down and their place was being taken (if at all) by night watchmen, supplemented in a few cases by day constables. Vast stretches of rural England went virtually unpoliced. The result was that, as in the riots provoked by John Wilkes in the 1760s, it was the army who were called upon to restore order.

It was mainly for this reason that forty barracks were built throughout England during the eighteenth century to house the soldiers and, perhaps more to the point, to prevent them being billeted with families they might later be ordered to control.

Yet unsatisfactory as this situation was, few challenged it. The most notable exception to this rule was the novelist and Bow Street magistrate, Henry Fielding, who published his *Enquiry into the Causes of the Late Increase of Robbers* deliberately to rouse the civil power from its lethargy. His report may not have been particularly original in its solutions but it skilfully sketched out the problems. Of these perhaps the most striking was the ease with which criminals escaped arrest. As Fielding noted, parts of London had become criminal sanctuaries where 'a rogue no sooner gives the alarm than twenty or thirty armed villains are ready to come to his assistance.' Henry Fielding died prematurely at the age of forty-seven and he was succeeded at Bow Street by his half brother John. Building on the foundation he inherited, John Fielding expanded the first body of 'real thief takers' into the Bow Street Runners and circulated regular information sheets on wanted criminals which eventually became the *Police Gazette*. He also tried to make the case for more general change, but with little more success than his brother.

Pleas for reform were largely ignored by the public and the chief response of Parliament was to set up a seemingly endless string of committees of inquiry. Giving evidence to one of these in 1770, John Fielding dismissed the watch as 'insufficient – their duty too hard – and their pay too small.' As for their organisation he reported that the 152 parish 'frontiers' were in such a confused state in London that the opposite sides of streets could lie in different parishes which generally meant that 'the watchmen on one side cannot lend assistance to persons on the other side.'³ Both arguments were to become familiar almost two centuries later when applied to police pay and police amalgamations, but at this stage they had little impact. The committee noted the upward trend in both robberies and burglaries; agreed that both crimes would increase even further unless effective action was taken; but declined to upset the traditional (and ineffective) methods employed. Ten years later, however, an event took place which did at last succeed in shaking the complacency of both public and Parliament.

The Gordon riots were the worst that London had ever suffered, even in the turbulence of the eighteenth century, and their violence has never been equalled since. In the course of a week, over three hundred were killed or wounded – a further twenty-five later perishing on the scaffold – and a vast number of houses and public buildings set on fire or destroyed. The riots took their name from Lord George Gordon, the fanatical leader of the extremist Protestant Association, who opposed a recent Act of Parliament which had relieved Catholics from various disabilities including the bar on enlisting in the army. Considering how badly British troops were faring at that time in the American War of Independence, it was a fairly dubious disability to have lifted. Nevertheless, the cause of 'no popery' had such emotive force that an enormous crowd, led by Gordon, marched on Westminster and virtually imprisoned Members of Parliament in the debating chamber. The siege was lifted by the intervention of the cavalry, but in the days which followed London was at the complete mercy of the mob.

In the East End, Catholic houses and chapels were destroyed; and the home of John Fielding, who was one of the few magistrates to try to intervene, was attacked and a bonfire made of the Fieldings' manuscripts. The Old Bailey was ransacked; at Newgate three hundred prisoners were released and three other London prisons were wrecked; and at Bloomsbury Square the home of the Lord Chief Justice was burnt down. Looting was widespread and the riots had such a traumatic effect on the Bank of England that a nightly picket was demanded from the army. In the end, of course, it was the army which saved London from even worse destruction. Nothing could have shown the complete irrelevance of the nightwatchmen system as the watchman seen at the height of the riots, lantern in hand, 'calling the hour as in time of profound tranquility.'

For the first time it seemed that the English might be prepared seriously to consider alternatives, and for the first time also the French police was seriously canvassed in Parliament as one of those alternatives. Speaking as the rioters were virtually firing

London at will, Lord Shelburne, who two years later became the first Home Secretary, tried to distinguish between the idea of an organised police and the way that the idea had been applied in France. He suggested that if members studied the Paris police they 'would find its construction excellent: its use and direction abominable. Let them embrace the one and shun the other.'[4] But the argument was too original for its time and as soon as the riots had run their course Parliament relapsed into its old lethargy, content with the government assurance that probably such disorder would not recur. The cause of police reform again seemed lost but a few years later, in 1785, Pitt introduced a Bill which was as radical as it was controversial.

The Bill – the London and Westminster Police Bill – recognised that some new initiative was needed. Introducing it, Sir Archibald MacDonald, the Solicitor General, observed that although the 'gallows groaned' with the executed, robbery not only continued but became ever more daring. 'No person,' the Solicitor General said, 'could feel himself unapprehensive of danger to the person or property if he walked the streets after it was dark.' The Government therefore had no intention of introducing new punishments but aimed to prevent crime by making detection more certain. The police which was to be formed would be under the control of three commissioners appointed by the Crown, and London was to be divided into nine divisions with a regular force of 'ministerial officers of peace' in each. It was in the drawing of these divisions that the government made its fatal mistake. For, without warning or consultation, the City suddenly found that it was to lose its independence and simply become a police division.

The City fathers reacted strongly and a petition which was presented to Parliament roundly condemned the Government for the double offence of seeking to create a force which was 'both new and arbitrary in the extreme' and complained that the new officers were to be given 'extraordinary and dangerous powers.' In the debate which followed, Alderman Townsend succinctly put the case of the City opponents. He declared himself ready at any time to enter upon a discussion of the causes of the increase in thefts which he diagnosed as a lack of adequate punishments. He lamented the shortage of suitable places for transportation; the undesirable judicial tendency not to hang for horse stealing; and complained that 'so strangely were men's feelings directed that thieves and robbers alone appeared to be fit objects of compassion in modern times.'[5]

The opposition was successful. Because of drafting defects, the bill had to be withdrawn and, answering questions on whether it would be reintroduced, the Prime Minister, Pitt, strangely confessed himself 'not to be perfectly master of the subject' and therefore not able to tell how well the new scheme would work in practice. The Solicitor General also back-pedalled furiously, and contented himself with assuring the House that he would have the bill printed so that members 'might take it with them into the country.' In fact, the bill was neither printed nor studied, and the first attempt to form a police force ended in humiliation. London had to wait for almost half a century before a further attempt was made – although the discarded bill did prove the basis of the Dublin Police Act of 1786 and the eventual formation of the Royal Irish Constabulary.

The years which followed could not have been worse chosen for the cause of police reform in England. The *ancien régime* in France had finally been swept away by the revolution of 1789 and in the first months of hope many of its most obnoxious devices went with it. *Lettres de cachet* were discontinued; censorship was abolished; and the mail was allowed to go free. The police were placed under the control of municipal committees and the brave claim was made that 'citizens will have none but citizens to govern them.' But neither liberalism nor citizen power survived long. The tide rapidly turned. In 1793 censorship was reimposed and seventy journalists and writers were executed. Thousands more perished in the reign of terror and revolutionary justice revealed itself as both more terrible and more efficient than even the system of the *ancien régime*. In the police names changed – the Royal Watch became the National Guard; and the *maréchaussé* became the *Gendarmerie Nationale* – but many of the same corrupt policemen continued to hold office, although one notable casualty was the last Lieutenant General, Thiroux de Crosne who, unwisely returning from exile in England, was promptly guillotined.

The control of the police very soon came out of the hands of local committees and in 1796 a new ministry was created – the Ministry of Police. The full significance of this step was not grasped immediately, mainly because of the ineffectiveness of the nine ministers who followed each other in rapid succession. In

1799, the tenth minister was appointed. At the time of his appointment Joseph Fouché was ambassador in the Netherlands, but he had made his reputation in the years of the terror which, even by those standards, was one of utter ruthlessness. In the years which followed Fouché exploited the full potential of a police used as an instrument of despotic rule.

Fouché's ministry of police took in not only Paris but the whole of France – and even extended into the empire which Napoleon was rapidly annexing. Paris became one of the four *arrondissements* of France and, although Napoleon saw the Prefect of Paris as a counterbalance to Fouché, there was no doubt that the prefect was very much the junior partner. In his ten years as minister, Fouché perfected the machine which had served the kings and which the revolution, as one of its prime aims, had sought to destroy. The *mouchards* became the *observateurs de l'esprit public,* but all this meant in practice was that their role had been extended. As before, they were paid by each denunciation, although some now received regular payments from Fouché's closest collaborator, Pierre Marie Desmarest, the head of the secret police. As well as spying, they were also required to act as *agents provocateurs* to create the conspiracies and disturbances which alone could show Fouché's ministry to its best advantage. The difficulty in Napoleonic France soon became whom to trust. Desmarest was probably used by Napoleon to spy on Fouché, and it was even rumoured (although never substantiated) that Josephine was used as a *mouchard domestique* to spy on Napoleon. The business was perhaps brought to its ultimate conclusion by Fouché's successor, the Duc de Rovigo who, not content with servants spying on their masters, employed masters to spy on their servants.

Other measures of repression were followed with the same thoroughness. The police controlled the press to such effect that, within twelve months of coming to office, Fouché had reduced the number of political journals from seventy-three to eleven. The post was once again being opened, and methods of recording information were brought to such a state of perfection that one writer has dubbed it the 'golden age of the dossier.'[6] Justice was remodelled and the *mesure de haute police* took the place of the *lettre de cachet,* which Fouché used to hold men whom the courts might mistakenly acquit, or for retaining prisoners whose sentences had expired. Corruption also prospered. The first secretary general of the police, Thurot, was sentenced to twelve years for fraud, and Fouché, who remained unconvicted, became one of the richest men in France. The police continued to raise their costs from a tax on gaming – to which was added a tax on prostitution.

Given both the example of the police just across the Channel and feelings roused by the Napoleonic wars, it seems remarkable that any progress was made at all in England. Yet these years were not altogether wasted. The Middlesex Justices Act of 1792 established new magistrates' offices in London to which paid constables were to be attached. The Act also brought to London Patrick Colquhoun as one of the new stipendiary magistrates. Colquhoun was then forty-seven, and had already a successful business career behind him in Glasgow, where at the age of thirty-seven he had been elected Lord Provost of the city. Following in the steps of the Fieldings, Colquhoun became a campaigning magistrate and his *Treatise on the Police of the Metropolis*, which ran through no less than eight editions, won him a national reputation.

To add force to his arguments, Colquhoun tried to measure the crime problem which London faced. He estimated that out of a population of one million there were 115,000 Londoners who supported themselves 'by pursuits either criminal, illegal or immoral.' His figures were clearly open to challenge, but this was less important than that the public were ready to believe them, seeing all around them ample evidence of all three pursuits. Like the Fieldings then, Colquhoun sought to arouse the public but, unlike them, he defined what he meant by police and became the first English writer to give police its modern meaning. His argument was that in England the police should be considered as a new science, not concerned with judicial powers leading to punishment but in preventing and detecting crimes and in preserving public order. Such a police system did not conflict with the liberty of the individual; on the contrary, as the police was the only effective way of restraining delinquency and thus protecting the public, it was a prerequisite of it. He might have made this last point more persuasively had he omitted his reference to the French police organisation as having reached the 'greatest degree of perfection' – an observation which so impressed the French that they had the treatise translated at a time when the two countries were locked in combat.

Colquhoun also added other novel and highly controversial proposals. He believed, for example, that the police should be able to pick out of the prison population the most dangerous criminals and syphon them off, by means of transportation to New South Wales. Nevertheless, his central idea of a preventive police under the dual control of the parish and a central board under the Home Secretary appeared at one stage to be on the verge of adoption. It was broadly endorsed by a Parliamentary committee of 1798 and Colquhoun prepared a draft bill. But then suddenly the whole matter was abandoned. Seventeen years later Colquhoun gave evidence to yet another select committee on the police and confirmed that it had been the government's intention to legislate. No reason had ever been advanced to him why the idea was dropped and he added sadly that he could 'never sufficiently lament' the change of heart.

It was 1811 before there was any serious renewal of pressure, and this time it was based, not on the campaign of a reforming magistrate, but on a series of murders in the East End just before Christmas. In the first series of murders on 7 December the whole Marr family, who ran a small shop in the Ratcliffe Highway in Wapping, were slaughtered with the ripping chisel of a ship's carpenter. Twelve days later the same murderer struck again, this time killing three and leaving his victims with their throats cut and their skulls fractured. A press and public outcry followed and in the panic that ensued almost fifty suspects (mainly foreigners) were held for questioning. In fact, the murderer turned out to be a Danish seaman, who hanged himself while awaiting questioning: and although defeating the hangman, he did not quite beat the Home Office, who had his body paraded through the East End in an attempt to placate the local population.[7] Once again, however, the movement for change ran out of steam and the subsequent committee of investigation confined itself to trying to improve the night watch. The prevailing attitude was still that of one writer who observed (from a point of safety): 'I had rather half a dozen people's throats were cut in Ratcliffe Highway every three or four years than be subject to domiciliary visits, spies and all the rest of Fouché's contrivances.'

The next years in England were the years of the inquiries. The inquiry of 1812 was followed by Parliamentary Inquiries in 1816, 1817 (when there were two), 1818, 1822, 1827, and 1828. It is possible to write off these committees as the prevarications of Governments anxious to avoid action, but this would be too easy.

Public and Parliament were at one. The public shared the opposition of the committee of 1818 to the French form of police. 'It would be a plan which would make every servant of every house a spy on the actions of his master, and all classes of society spies on each other.' They agreed with the committee of 1822 (chaired by none other than Sir Robert Peel) that 'It is difficult to reconcile an effective system of police with that perfect freedom of action and exemption from interference which are the greatest privileges and blessings of society in this country.' The committee simply reflected with striking phrases the public view.

Yet by the 1820s the long struggle of the English to avoid introducing a police force had silently entered its last stage. The Peterloo massacre, when order was put in the hands of the armed volunteers of the Manchester Yeomanry, was a recent memory and the toll of eleven dead and four hundred wounded had shocked not only liberal opinion but also some of the makers of policy in Parliament. While Colquhoun's view that the idea of police and the demands of freedom were not opposites had received influential support from Jeremy Bentham and the Utilitarians. Most important of all, there was now a Home Secretary who not only believed in reform but had the political skill to achieve it. The remarks of the 1822 committee had shown more of Robert Peel as a politician than as a police reformer. It would be too much to say that he believed in taking the public with him, but he recognized the value of avoiding head-on collisions. His style was one of the reasons that a measure, which had been resisted so strongly for so long, passed through Parliament virtually unchallenged and at a comparatively break-neck speed.

In 1828 Peel moved in the House of Commons for a further committee to examine the state of the police in London. Few who listened to him then could have guessed that it presaged change – 'I must confess that I am not very sanguine with respect to the benefits to be derived from this committee' – let alone fundamental reform. The committee took a mere six months to report. They were heavily influenced by one of Bentham's closest disciples Edwin Chadwick, whose evidence to the committee defined the police role in words which are strikingly similar to the instructions later issued to the new force: 'The first great object of a police, that to which every practical adoption should conduce, is to prevent the commission of crime. The second is when crime has been committed to detect and to bring to conviction the perpetrators of it.'

In its report the committee considered there 'was a strong presumption in favour of material change in the system of police' and proposed the setting up of a police office for London which would be under the control of the Home Secretary. Peel readily accepted the Report and after some months of careful preparation introduced the Metropolis Police Improvement Bill on 15 April 1829.

His approach was again deceptively low key, and he was careful not to court arguments of principle. The first part of his speech was taken up with a determinedly dull exposition of the size of the crime problem, showing that London was under greater challenge than any other part of the country. He then went on to a scarcely more controversial criticism of the night watchman system which left parishes like Fulham entirely unguarded. Peel's view was that 'the chief requisites of an efficient police were unity of design and responsibility of its agents.' This he believed would be achieved by putting the agents of the police under the control of a Board of Police. The Board would be supervised by the Commissioners and the Commissioners would be responsible to the Home Secretary himself. Such a system he declared hopefully would remove the temptation to crime which the present lax system of police held out to criminals, and rather than threatening liberty it would enable people to live in 'liberty and peace' free from the threat of ever-increasing crime. There was a short debate but the Bill went through virtually without question.[8]

The Bill then went to the House of Lords and Peel wrote to the Duke of Wellington: 'I hardly know what objections may be made to the Bill as I have heard none in the Commons.' The Lords were no more critical than the Commons. Wellington duly repeated Peel's arguments and on 19 July, the Bill became law. On Tuesday, 29 September 1829, the first constables of the new force of three thousand appeared on the streets dignified in their tailed coats and top hats, and armed with no more than truncheons and rattles. Europe had never seen a force quite like it. One of their new commissioners, Richard Mayne, set out the aim. 'The primary object of an efficient police is the prevention of crime; the next that of detection and punishment of offenders against the peace.' This preventive police was to work with the co-operation of the public and Peel left his new constables in no doubt how this was to be won. He 'will be civil and obliging to all people of every rank and class . . . He must be particularly cautious not to interfere idly or unnecessarily in order to make a display of authority . . . He must remember that there is no qualification so indispensable to a police officer as a perfect command of temper.'

In London the initial battle was over. The new Metropolitan Police, with its headquarters at Scotland Yard, had to fight its first defensive battles of acceptance, but there was never any question that the police was there to stay. Elsewhere in England and Wales the long struggle continued. A local government measure of 1835 gave the boroughs the power to form regular forces, and the vital new centres created by the industrial revolution, like Birmingham and Manchester, formed their own forces once their position was recognized by charter. But in many parts of the country the reforms of Peel and the commissioners of the Metropolitan Police were just echoes – interesting but not relevant.

When a Royal Commission (which included among its members Edwin Chadwick and one of the new commissioners Charles Rowan) reported in 1839, they painted a horrifying picture.[9] In contradiction to Peel the commission found that the proportions of 'habitual depredators and other criminals' to the population was highest not in London, but in towns like Newcastle-on-Tyne, Bristol and even stately Bath. They discovered that, although towns with regular police forces did well – one criminal reported Manchester as 'the worst town in England for a thief' – other areas were apparently lawless. One prisoner giving evidence said that he had seen thieves rescued from the hands of the authorities by other thieves, and of professional criminals who had been living by crime for year after year virtually undetected.

It was not surprising then that the commission's solution was radical. They rejected the idea of a police force divided into separate divisions as clearly inefficient, and instead proposed a national force under one executive authority. Periodically the policemen in this force would change from district to district, and the force would have a mobile reserve of between three and four hundred which would be ready for emergencies. They rejected any constitutional argument against a national force and argued that the way to maintain the freedom of the subject was 'not to render the authorities impotent but to make them strictly responsible for the

26

use of power with which they may be invested.' They dismissed the French police as political rather than preventive, and added: 'The chief and proper objection to the police forces abroad are that they act on powers which are arbitrary, the force which we propose could only act on powers which are legal and for which they would be responsible to in the Courts of Law and ultimately to Parliament.'

It was a remarkably modern argument, but the challenge of the report was never taken up. The Whig Government, beset by problems with the Chartists, and needing the help of the magistrates to contain them, jibbed at such fundamental reform. Instead, they introduced an Act which did just what the commission had said would be inefficient and enabled magistrates to establish professional but local forces. Even then they did not compel the magistrates to form forces, but only 'if they should think it necessary.' Thus the Bill bore little or no resemblance to the report – although it was enough to provoke the young Disraeli into describing it as a 'considerable civil revolution in the country'.

Judged by the standards of revolution the effect was startlingly incomplete. When a select committee came to review progress in 1853[10] they found twenty counties and two Ridings of Yorkshire without a county police, and a further seven with a police only partially established. According to the Home Office this meant that about half the whole surface of England and Wales was without an efficient police. (Scotland was more advanced with only four counties without a police force). Clearly the unpoliced areas would have to be brought up to scratch and it was Lord Palmerston, now briefly at the Home Office, who had to decide how this should be done. Like his predecessors, Peel and Sir John Russell, Palmerston would have favoured a national force, but he saw clearly enough the limits placed by the politically possible.

Instead he proposed an organization which because it meant the disappearance of the small borough forces was no more politically acceptable. It took three attempts to get reform through and by this time Palmerston was Prime Minister. The small borough forces remained, all the counties were required to establish forces, and the Home Office was able to advise on efficiency through three inspectors. Thus by 1856 the legal foundation at any rate had been laid for a uniform system of police – although the Metropolitan

Police remained (and still remains) the only force coming directly under the authority of the Home Secretary.

It is easy to ridicule the eighteenth- and nineteenth-century Englishman's fear of a police. In retrospect, however, it may well be that this long painful process was itself one of the major reasons for the English police's later success. Governments were forced to tread carefully and realized that they were most vulnerable to the charge that the police infringed the liberty of the individual. The police were thus made accountable to the public, the Courts and Parliament. The police themselves fully realized the suspicion that the public harboured and must have had a fairly shrewd idea which way a Government would jump in any conflict between police and public. In Parliament it was attacks on the police rather than support for them, which was the popular cause in the early years.

The French police was fundamentally different. It had always had a political function and was thus supported, almost automatically, by the Government, as it was operating in their interests. Its standards were the standards of the Government in power. Public goodwill was largely irrelevant and public respect came mostly from fear of its efficiency. As Leon Radzinowicz has put it, the French police was a force superimposed on the public and not accountable to it. Added to this, there was public cynicism about whether the French police would ever change. The police of the *ancien régime* had given way to the police of the Revolution: and the police of Napoleon had given way to the police of the Restoration. Yet nothing greatly had altered – unless it was that with each new stage the police became more intrusive and the use of spies more widespread. Such then was the tradition of the French police.

The English police on the other hand were introduced with reluctance, and even then viewed with suspicion. This meant that reform was slow, and that the national force wanted in the name of efficiency by Home Secretaries from Peel to Palmerston was never introduced – but it did mean from the outset that the English police were forced to win public trust.

2

The Making of
a Police State

The Great War, which came to an end in 1918 with the defeat of
Germany, is often taken to have ushered in a new and violent era
in Europe marking a decisive break with the well ordered past.
Such a generalization may be historically convenient but it hardly
applies to all European countries with equal force. In Britain the
past had not been noticeably well ordered and the years immediately before the war had seen a resurgence of violence comparable
to the Chartist disturbances seventy years before. In Tonypandy
troops were brought in to prevent a miners' strike getting out of
hand; in Liverpool a policeman was kicked to death and several
hundred injured in riots; while political militants appeared in the
unlikely shape but undoubted violence of suffragettes seeking the
vote for women. In contrast, the period following the war was comparatively peaceful in spite of all the talk of the imminence of
Bolshevist revolution. The red flag did manage to get itself raised
briefly over Glasgow town hall but the characteristic unrest was not
political but industrial. The railwaymen, the miners and even
some of the police went on strike – but the authorities were rarely
in serious trouble. Even when the potentially explosive General
Strike was called in 1926, order was easily maintained and in a
symbolic match at Plymouth the police played the strikers at
football. The public and the strikers applied their own discipline
and in the main violence was avoided.

In Germany the progression was very different: the new era of
violence visible to all. The trauma of defeat had been made all the
more hard to bear by its almost complete surprise. The German
public knew little of their armies' conclusive reverses in the autumn
of 1918 and even when the peace was signed in November the army
remained silent about the inevitability of surrender. The political

leaders of the new Weimar Republic were saddled with the dishonour and blame of defeat and almost immediately dubbed 'the November criminals'. The fiction was allowed to develop that the gallant army at the front had been stabbed in the back by the politicians at home. Parties who rejected the peace and aimed to restore Germany to her rightful place among nations were assured of a wide appeal and, as national inflation was succeeded by international depression, the extremists triumphed, democracy collapsed and a new and terrible police state emerged. The crimes of that police state are well known. Nothing is gained by listing them once more for the plain fact is that the excesses of any police state vary only in number and degree. A more interesting question is whether the police of the Weimar Republic could have prevented the rise of Hitler? Should a police service in a democracy be able to prevent the overthrow of that democracy?

On the face of it the Republic could boast a powerful police. In strength it totalled a massive two hundred thousand including a permanent reserve held in barracks ready to deal with exactly the kind of riots, intimidation and violence which characterized these years. Yet this strength was more apparent than real. A well meaning constitution laid down that Federal police powers could only be exercised in the direst emergency and even then for only a very limited time. The real control of the police was exercised, not by the Federal Government but by the separate states (*Länder*) of which the most important were Prussia and Bavaria and by those large cities like Berlin and Munich which were allowed their own forces. In the states power was shared by the Minister of the Interior who was responsible for the day-to-day running of the force, and the Minister of Justice who not only supervised the investigation of crimes but was ultimately responsible for whether prosecutions took place. It was an arrangement which left the national Government dangerously weak and it was made no easier by the dubious loyalty to the Republic of some of the police themselves.

In Berlin the police president was deeply implicated in the Kapp Putsch in 1920 which sought to overthrow the Government and replace it by one of the extreme right; and in Munich it was Pöhner, the police president of the city, who when asked if he was aware that there were political murder gangs operating in Bavaria replied 'Yes, but not enough of them.' Yet such examples should not be exaggerated. There is no evidence to suggest that in the years when Hitler was building up his strength the police *generally* were either disloyal to the Republic or riddled with Nazi sympathizers. The position was rather that at several crucial points the police provided the evidence which could have stopped Hitler dead in his tracks but that tragically these opportunities were never taken. All too often the efforts of the police ran into the ground because of the weakness of ministers in refusing to act or because of the obvious partiality of the courts.

The judges operated an undoubted double standard of justice openly based on politics. Frequently the political offenders of the left – who admittedly posed as big a problem up to 1930 as the Nazis – received long prison sentences while the extremists of the right who sought to overthrow the Republic itself were treated with incredible leniency. A clear example came after the collapse of the Kapp Putsch. During the rebellion the notorious Ehrhardt Brigade*, had occupied Berlin enabling Doctor Wolfgang Kapp to proclaim himself Chancellor and forcing the President of the Republic and the Government to flee. Part of the German army under General von Lüttwitz supported the rebellion and the situation was saved only by a General Strike of the trade unions. Over seven hundred were put on trial for their part in the *putsch* but out of this enormous total only one – the Police President of Berlin – was sentenced and then only to five years' 'honorary confinement.' When a Prussian Court ordered that his pension should be withdrawn, the Supreme Court ordered it to be restored. As for General von Lüttwitz who had fled to Hungary, a kindly German Court later ordered back payments of his pension to include the time when he was successfully evading justice. Such then was the penalty for treason meted out by the Courts.

In Bavaria the Courts also played a discreditable part. In the years following the war, Bavaria in general and Munich in particular became the natural home for the disaffected elements of the Republic. Adolf Hitler was beginning to build up his National Socialist Party and the members of the disbanded free corps found

---

* One of the armed bands of volunteers (*Freikorps*) formed immediately after the war when the regular army (*Reichswehr*) was restricted in number to one hundred thousand by the Allies. Ostensibly they were to protect the eastern frontier of Germany against attack but they also provided ready recruits for any attempt to overthrow the German Republic.

an outlet for their energies in the party's brown shirted storm troops (*Sturmabteilung* or SA). In the army in Bavaria were men like Captain Ernst Röhm who was later to lead the SA. For a time, Pöhner was the police president of Munich and his assistant was Wilhelm Frick, later to become Hitler's Minister of the Interior; and at the Ministry of Justice there was Franz Gürtner who eventually became Hitler's Minister of Justice. The traditional separatism of the Bavarians themselves and their hostility to rule from Berlin added to the dangerous weakness of the Government. It was this weakness which Hitler set out to exploit.

His first serious opportunity came in 1923 when the French occupation of the Ruhr outraged German opinion and accelerated even further the catastrophic drop in value of the Mark. In Bavaria power rested with a triumvirate consisting of Gustav von Kahr, a right wing monarchist who was the State Commissioner; General Otto von Lossow, the army commander in Bavaria; and Colonel Hans von Seisser, the head of the State police. Hitler's plan was to win their support and to proclaim a National Government, and (emulating Mussolini in Italy) to march on Berlin. After several false starts Hitler took his chance on the night of 8 November when Kahr was due to address a meeting at the Bürgerbraükeller, a large beer hall in the south east of Munich. Surrounding the hall with his storm troops, Hitler broke into the meeting and attracting attention by firing his pistol into the air, told the startled audience that army and police barracks had been occupied by his own men. Thanks to Frick the police in the hall were under orders not to intervene and Kahr, Lossow and Seisser were hustled into a side room. There they were persuaded by General Ludendorff (a distinguished war leader and implacable opponent of the Republic) to co-operate and in an apparent show of unity the new National Government was proclaimed to a now enthusiastic audience. But this shotgun unity did not outlive the emotion of the meeting.

When it broke up Hitler's three necessary allies – representing the State, the army and the police – were allowed to slip away. Kahr immediately moved his Government to Regensburg and renounced the agreement with Hitler as null and void. Röhm, who had occupied the War Ministry building, now found himself surrounded by the army; and Pöhner who went off to take control of the police headquarters, was promptly arrested. Faced with what had become a desperate situation Hitler had no real alternative but to agree to Ludendorff's suggestion that they should march into Munich and take over the departments of Government – a desperate plan based on the assumption that neither the army nor the police (who included many ex-servicemen) would fire on a column led by Ludendorff.

At about 11.00 am on the morning of 9 November the column of three thousand storm troopers led by Hitler and Ludendorff and including other later Nazi leaders like Göring, Hess and Himmler set off. For the police, who had been given the task of stopping the column, there were two natural strategic points. The first was the Ludwig Bridge which spans the River Isar but here Göring forced a passage by threatening to shoot the hostages he was holding. The second point was the narrow funnel formed by the Residenzstrasse which leads to the wide square of the Odeonsplatz and the goal of the War Ministry. What mattered here was not numbers but the control of the neck of the funnel. It was exactly at this point that the detachment of armed police were positioned and this time they stood firm. A shot was fired (probably from the column) and it was immediately followed by volleys from both sides. Sixteen Nazis and three policemen were killed and many others, including Göring, were injured. Only Ludendorff and his adjutant kept their nerve and marched on steadily through the police line but they were entirely alone. The Nazi leaders fled in panic and two days later Hitler was arrested. The beer hall Putsch had apparently ended in ignominious failure.

Yet anyone who imagined that the action of the police had put an end to Hitler's career reckoned without the intervention of the courts. Extraordinarily, the trial proved to be little more than a platform for Hitler. Watched for the first time by the World's press, he was permitted to explain his policies at length virtually without check from the presiding judge who only intervened to silence open applause in the court room. He was allowed to cross examine at will; to interrupt witnesses particularly Kahr, Lossow and Seisser who appeared in the vulnerable roles of prosecution witnesses; and to openly attack the police whom he claimed had stained their record by enforcing the law. The law itself was clear. Under the German Penal Code 'attempts to alter by force the constitution of the German Reich or any German State shall be punished by life long imprisonment.' In the event Ludendorff was acquitted altogether and Hitler was sentenced to five years' imprisonment with an assurance that he would be eligible for parole after six months.

To their credit the police did not allow the matter to rest there. Alarmed at the prospect of parole, two reports were sent by the director of the Bavarian state police to the Ministry of the Interior on 8 May and 22 September 1924.[1] Both reports opposed parole but suggested that if parole was granted that Hitler, who was an Austrian citizen, should be deported. They warned of the alternative: 'The moment he is set free Hitler will, because of his energy, again become the driving force of new serious public riots and a continual menace to the security of the State.' As a result of the reports, the Bavarian State Attorney filed formal complaints opposing parole but at this point the Minister of Justice, Gürtner, intervened and the complaints were withdrawn. On 20 December Hitler was released having served a mere nine months of his sentence. The following year he renounced his Austrian citizenship to reduce the chances of deportation – although he did not finally become a German citizen until 1932.

The chief effect on Hitler of the collapse of the beer hall Putsch was to turn him away from the tactics of sudden revolution. Instead his new policy became to work for power apparently within the confines of the constitution, although entirely committed to its overthrow. He did not now seek to defeat the police on the streets but to acquire by political means the legal power to give the police (and the other Government services) their orders. This time members of the party laid low waiting for their opportunity.* These were much more dangerous tactics but again they could have been defeated by firm action. The thin protective covering of legality with which Hitler tried to surround the party scarcely disguised the fact that he was building up a private, well disciplined force which presented a fundamental challenge to the State itself.

Hitler already had his storm troops but they were an unreliable political instrument. The ambitions of many of the SA leaders was to become part of a new stronger Germany and, from Hitler's point of view, they were all too often content to play soldiers and try to recapture the comradeship of the Great War. The answer which Hitler found to this problem was to form a *corps d'élite* within the

---

* The police had their share of secret Nazis – a notable example being Artur Hebe of the Prussian Criminal Police who later became an SS general.

SA sworn to absolute obedience to himself. The new group was called the *Schutzstaffel* (SS) and in 1929 Hitler appointed Heinrich Himmler, who was then twenty-eight and earning his living as a poultry farmer, to lead it. For his part, Himmler recruited a cashiered naval officer, Reinhard Heydrich, even younger than himself to form an intelligence unit (*Sicherheitsdienst* or SD) within the SS: an elite within the elite. In the meantime, Hitler had also brought back his old friend Captain Ernst Röhm who had been serving with the Bolivian Army, to reorganize and strengthen the storm troops themselves. Röhm and his SA were to have a profound effect in the final violence of Hitler's rise to power while Himmler and Heydrich were to weld the SS into just the kind of efficient force of organized terror which Hitler required to bring Germany to heel and later to dominate most of Europe.

Yet the evidence which could have put paid to these organizations had been carefully collected by the political section of the Prussian police.[2] In a massive report on the Nazi movement in 1930, the Prussian police identified the SA and the SS as the instruments of power of the Nazi party 'whose first duty was to carry out the planned overthrow of the Government.' They exposed the so-called 'sports' courses' for SA leaders by showing that the content of the courses included rifle training and tactics during engagements; and they described the para-military organization of the SA with its military ranks and its directive on discipline that 'SA men must implicitly obey their leaders.' On Hitler's policy of legality the police report commented:

> The significance which may be attached to these declarations by a revolutionary army movement has been pointed out by Reich Supreme Court in its numerous high treason cases against members of the K.P.D. [German Communist Party] in which it characterises the frequent declarations of legality on the part of the Communists as completely unreliable assertions made for their own protection.

The report warned:

> . . . there is a systematic campaign against the foundations of public order. This campaign aims to and is equipped to endanger the constitutional State and thus is equipped to prepare the ground for the complete rebuilding of the constitutional structure as planned by the NSDAP [Nazi party]. All the activities

of the NSDAP – its press, its meetings, its propaganda, and the activities of its members in the parliaments of the Reich, the States and the communities – are consciously, systematically and persistently dedicated to this goal.

As if this was not enough the report also detailed the Nazis' attempts to win over both serving members of the army and the police to their cause. They concluded that the Nazi party was an organization whose activities constituted 'an undertaking of high treason' clearly laying its members open to prosecution.

Nothing could have been clearer than the warning and nothing more typical than the response. The report first went through normal Government channels to the Reich Attorney General, Karl Werner, in the summer of 1930 and in August Dr Kempner, the chief legal officer of the Prussian police, followed this up by publishing an anonymous article in the legal journal, *Die Justiz*, summarizing the report and calling on the Attorney General to enforce the law. The article was forwarded to the Attorney General and eventually, in January 1931, Werner replied that it was being investigated. Other reminders were sent throughout 1931 but all received the same reply that the investigation was continuing and was 'not fully completed.' Finally in August 1932 – over two years after the report had reached him – Werner announced his decision not to prosecute. The Reich Attorney General (a Nazi sympathizer who continued in office when Hitler came to power) had successfully used his position to prevent action being taken.

Yet in the final analysis, the blame for the failure to act lay not with the Courts, nor with a few highly placed lawyers, but with the political leaders of the Weimar Republic. If the political will had existed the Nazis could have been smashed – but the political will did not exist. When in April 1932 the national Government finally brought itself to move against the Nazis and ban both the SA and the SS their resolution hardly outlived the publication of their decree. The decree recognized that the proscribed organizations amounted to 'a private army whose very existence constitutes a state within a state.' Yet within days the close circle of advisers which surrounded President Hindenburg were seeking to lift the ban and intriguing against the men who had imposed it – the Chancellor, Heinrich Brüning, and his Minister of Defence, General Groener. In May the ban was debated in the Reichstag where Groener faced the wrath of the right and went down to defeat. Two days later he resigned. A few weeks later Brüning was dismissed and on 16 June the ban was lifted. The result was immediate and bloody. There was bitter street fighting between storm troopers and the Communists and, according to Albert Grzesinski, the Police President of Berlin, in seven weeks eighty-two people were killed and four hundred seriously wounded in Prussia alone.[3] The funerals of the SA men who perished in the riots became the occasion for further Nazi demonstrations and during one of these at Altona, near Hamburg, nineteen people were killed.

The new Chancellor was Franz von Papen who owed his position to General von Schleicher – a master of intrigue who had done most to destroy the previous administration. The approach of Papen and Schleicher to the Nazis was based on the disastrous premise that politically they could outgun Hitler and could use his popular support to their own advantage. It was in pursuit of this policy that in July 1932 Papen deposed the Prussian government – made up of a Social Democrat and centre party coalition – and declared himself Reich commissioner for Prussia. The pretext for the *coup* was that the Prussian government had shown itself unable to deal firmly with the Communists during the Altona riots; but the real reason was that Papen hoped to appease the Nazis by this show of authoritarianism and gather for himself some 'anti-Marxist' credit. He sought to outmanoeuvre Hitler, ignoring the clear danger that if he failed he could pass to Hitler control of Germany's most important state – including its strongest police force – unfettered by democratic checks. Faced with this challenge, it was next the will of the political leaders of the centre which failed. In 1920 the Kapp Putsch had been defeated by a general strike and that option was open again, but unhappily there was virtually no resistance. The Minister of the Interior, Carl Severing, passed over control of the police (after a token show of force by Papen) and the leaders of the force were led away to a brief internment. If a *coup* could be so easily accomplished, then the final collapse of the Republic could not be long delayed.

In January 1933 Hitler became Chancellor and almost immediately his concept of the police role became evident. The Prussian police law, which was drafted as late as 1931, had placed on the police a general responsibility to take measures to protect the general public and the individual citizen 'within the law'. Such ideas were entirely alien to the new Prussian Minister of the Interior,

Hermann Göring who, as part of the political bargain agreed by Hitler, now assumed control of a force which policed two-thirds of Germany. Two weeks after he took office at the end of January, Göring issued his first instructions to the force. The police were warned to avoid any show of hostility to the SA and SS, who contained the most 'constructive national elements.' The directive continued—'Police officers who make use of firearms in the execution of their duties will, without regard to the consequences of such use, benefit by my protection; those who, out of a misplaced regard for such consequences fail in their duty will be punished.' Göring was concerned only with constructing a political police to enforce the Nazi will by whatever means were necessary.

To achieve this, Göring set about changing the policemen. Although regular policemen continued to serve, the top ranks of the Prussian police were almost entirely replaced.[4] The new head of the police became the SS General Kurt Daluege and he was surrounded by other members of the SA and SS. Göring next recruited no less than fifty thousand police auxiliaries, who again were mainly SA and SS men and who immediately appeared on duty with white arm bands over their brown or black uniform. A further sinister development was the appointment of Rudolf Diels (one of the regular policemen to survive the purge) to head a new department of the Prussian political police – Department IA. It was Diels' job to build up a private intelligence system for Göring and shortly the new department was to be officially named *Geheimestaatspolizei* – Secret State Police or Gestapo.[5] In Prussia Hitler's tactics of building up his own private forces ready to take over when the opportunity came had paid off.

Away from Berlin in Bavaria, Himmler had also been hard at work. When he had taken over the SS in 1929 there had been fewer than three hundred members; by the time Hitler became Chancellor there were some fifty thousand placed throughout Germany. Heydrich had similarly built up the SD and already screened the Bavarian political police to see which men might be useful after a *putsch*. In Bavaria the *putsch* came on 9 March and as a result Himmler became the new head of the Bavarian police. The remaining stages of the Nazi revolution quickly followed. The Reichstag fire in Berlin was Hitler's opportunity to issue his ill named decree for 'the protection of the people and the state', which restricted the freedom of both the public and the press. On 21 March, following an election in which the Nazis failed to get an absolute majority, but nevertheless polled seventeen million votes, a law was passed which in effect did away with the constitution. By stages the state assemblies were dissolved, opposition parties banned, and trade unions made illegal. Unmistakable signs of the new Nazi society appeared – like the concentration camp opened at Dachau.

It was in fact Göring who set up the earliest concentration camps but it was Himmler who developed them. Himmler set up his first concentration camp at Dachau on 22 March 1933. Under the order establishing the camp, men and women could be taken into 'protective custody' for no other reason than suspicion of activities inimical to the state. A few months later, Himmler was to lay down a further directive:

> The term commitment to a concentration camp is to be openly announced as 'until further notice' . . . In certain cases the Reichfuhrer S.S. and Chief of the German police will order flogging in addition to detention in a concentration camp . . . In this case too there is no objection to spreading the rumour of this increased punishment to add to the deterrent effect.

Himmler saw Dachau as the model concentration camp and certainly it was a clear guide of what was to come. To control the camp Himmler established a volunteer formation of SS men (accurately called the Death's Head unit) and among the first volunteers to serve at Dachau were Adolf Eichmann and Rudolf Hoess who later ran Auschwitz. A terrible new weapon was being welded for the police state which was now almost complete.

What lessons can we draw for the police from the Nazi revolution? Certainly it is clear that a police force can only operate effectively provided there is an effective law enforcement system. This does not mean that the courts should be servants of the police (that is the badge of the police state) but it does mean that the law should be capable of being enforced. The prosecuting authority must be prepared to bring a case when provided with clear evidence. The courts must be prepared to convict on the evidence and award meaningful sentences. Yet an even more important lesson of Weimar is the dependence of the police on political support and leadership. Practically no determined political action against the Nazis was ever taken. Politicians like Schleicher and

Papen thought that they could manipulate Hitler; the Communists kept up their attacks on the Social Democrats and so split the working class opposition; and the army – the final arbiter of German politics – remained neutral as long as Hitler followed his policy of legality and did not attempt a *putsch*. It was political weakness and political miscalculation which above all gave Hitler his opportunity.

Of course the police of the Weimar Republic were not blameless, but nevertheless it is difficult to see how they could have achieved very much more than they did. A police force operating inside a democracy is not an independent agency: it cannot enforce the law by itself. As Professor Sir Alan Bullock puts it: 'The major lesson of 1930 to 1933 is that when a country is faced with a revolutionary challenge, what is needed is resolute *political leadership*. The police can only act effectively in so far as the Government and the political system provides such leadership.'

3

The Tactics of Provocation

On the face of it the Nazi occupation of Europe would have seemed certain to have led to fierce public hostility to the police forces which were reconstructed once the War ended. The association between police power and the restrictions of the War years would have appeared too uncomfortably close. Yet strangely this was not always the case. In Germany and Italy hostility to the police was strong but in other countries the atrocities and brutalities of the Nazis were identified with the Nazis themselves and generally did not rub off on the national police forces. Certainly it was true that some policemen had remained in their jobs throughout the War and had actively collaborated – but collaboration had not been confined to the police. Equally it was true that other policemen had risked, and lost their lives in the struggle for liberation. In Paris over two hundred policemen had been killed in August 1944 in the bitter street fighting with German troops which preceded the allies' advance. Other French policemen had been active members of the resistance movement.* Nor were the French police alone in providing active opposition to the Germans. In Denmark the Nazis were so concerned about the help that the police would give in the allies' advance that they rounded up two thousand and sent them to concentration camps. The policemen who escaped the net joined the resistance movement. While in tiny Luxembourg the police who refused to co-operate were deported.

Many policemen then had shared with the public the hardships

---

* One British Agent who was helped by the French police was Neil Marten, now the Conservative MP for Banbury. A member of Special Operations Executive (SOE) working with the French resistance, Marten had lost his own identity documents and was provided with a replacement set by the police in Lyons.

and demands of occupation and partly this explained the acceptance of the police once the War had ended. An even more powerful reason was the understandable demand for order in a Europe which had experienced the full chaos of war. But even so this demand for order was not unlimited. Europe had changed. A new concern about individual liberty and a fear of abuse of power sprang naturally from people who had seen their own liberties trampled in the dirt. On this the middle classes and the middle aged felt as deeply as the young students who had been society's traditional conscience. The police were accepted provided that they were seen to be acting within their powers but public loyalty could not be taken for granted. The police response had to be seen to match the threat and with the growth of television many more of the public than ever before could see for themselves the police performance.

In the immediate years of European recovery these problems were muted. During the Fifties there were large demonstrations, like the marches organized by the supporters of nuclear disarmament, but these were usually peaceful and presented no real difficulties for the police. But by the beginning of the Sixties there were the unmistakable rumbles of the approaching storm. One such warning came in Munich in 1962. The occasion was a loud and boisterous concert in the student area of Schwabing in the city. When the students refused to leave the hall at the official close of the concert, the caretaker called in the police to remove them. To achieve this the police sent a lone patrol car and four policemen but the only result was that the police car had its tyres let down and the concert spilled over into the Leopoldstrasse outside. The police then went to exactly the opposite extreme and sent in mounted police to clear the streets. The press took the side of the students and the next night there were fresh disturbances. For the police the whole operation had been a disaster. Their initial force had been too small to carry out its role even assuming that the role itself was correct: while the follow up appeared to be a hopeless over reaction to a number of boisterous students. The lessons of the Munich incident could usefully have been studied by the police of Amsterdam for it was there that a much more serious challenge came four years later. This was presented by a group dubbed the *Provos*.

The *Provos* took their name from the French word *provocateur* but even today in Holland there is no general agreement about what they were setting out to do. It was certainly true that they believed in constructive political action – and indeed five of them were later elected to the Amsterdam Council. It was true that they were left wing but equally they detested – and were detested by – the Communists. It was true that they aimed at disruption but they opposed violence – although unable to control the violence their disruption caused. Yet in spite of all their contradictions the *Provos* did have a philosophy. This was perhaps put best by one of their leaders, Rob Stolk:

> Our aim is to reactivate democracy. There is no real democracy in Holland, Britain or France. They are always saying you are free to demonstrate and to say and do what you like but we are proving it isn't true. Everything we do is democratic, something we have the right to do – and we land in jail for it. We are a kind of motor, a catalyst for a more democratic society.[1]

There was of course nothing new in the aim for a more democratic society but the particular tactics adopted by the *Provos* to achieve it could claim to be innovative.

The *Provos* did not appeal to public opinion with massive demonstrations nor did they challenge the power of the state in direct confrontation. Instead they chose to tweak the tail of the authorities in a more or less playful way and wait for the response. Their hope was that the authorities would over react or respond in a way which would make them seem absurd. Facing the brunt of these tactics of gentle provocation were the most obvious representatives of the authorities, the police. 1966 became the year of 'the happenings'. The groups of students and other young people which Amsterdam attracts like a magnet came together for spontaneous events staged either in the street or on Spui Square in the middle of the city. The 'happenings' usually amounted to no more than fifty or one hundred young people gathering in a circle, clapping hands and singing songs. Nevertheless, even such apparently harmless behaviour – which may have been unusual but was hardly illegal – served its purpose. The small groups attracted crowds of onlookers waiting for 'something to happen' and in this atmosphere trivial incidents could spark off serious violence. The very fact that the behaviour was unusual prompted police investigation and once there was investigation there came the problem of how the police should respond. It was here that the Amsterdam police were frequently led into major error.

An outstanding example was the case of Koosje Koster. Miss Koster managed to attract an evening crowd in Amsterdam by doing no more than giving away raisins. There were about two hundred taking part in the free distribution and perhaps another thousand onlookers. Those at the back of the crowd pushed forward to see what was happening and eventually the police decided it was their job to find out also. Having reached the front, the police decided that rather than lose face (and certainly rather than accept the proffered raisins) they should take away Miss Koster. She resisted passively and the scene ended with Miss Koster being carried away feet first by the police for no other reason than she had been guilty of 'disturbing the peace' by distributing free raisins. The news spread quickly and an hour later there was a full scale riot. Another instance was the wedding in March 1966 of Crown Princess Beatrix to her German husband Claus von Amsberg. In this case the *Provos* capitalized on the strong anti German feeling in Amsterdam which had suffered particularly badly at the hands of the Nazis.* During the wedding procession the *Provos* threw smoke bombs and although few of the bombs landed anywhere near the couple's golden coach mounted policemen wielding truncheons were sent in to deal with the demonstrators. As the Special Correspondent of *The Times* noted 'the police reacted strongly – too strongly in the view of some people here.' Once again it was widely held that the police response had been out of proportion to the challenge.

The affair of Princess Beatrix's wedding served only as a prelude to much greater disturbances in June. During an industrial dispute one thousand building workers marched on the city hall in protest at deductions made from their summer holiday bonus. There were clashes with the police in which a building worker fell dead and (although post mortem examination showed that he had died from a heart attack) the Communists blamed the police. A one day strike was called and building workers marched on the offices of the Conservative newspaper *De Telegraaf* which they claimed had not truthfully reported the earlier demonstration. Windows were broken

---

* Even today fierce public opposition prevents the release of three German war criminals who have been held in Holland since the War and have grown old in prison.

and delivery vans set on fire and the building workers then marched to Dam Square. Here there were pitched battles with the police who used tear gas and made repeated charges to clear the Square. The disturbances had now become full scale riots and others joined in besides the building workers. Barricades were quickly thrown up in the centre of the city; pavements torn up; and one car load of demonstrators tore through the city's streets hurling rocks through store windows. The next night three thousand demonstrators stoned the police and continued on a path of destruction through the city breaking windows and tearing up traffic meters. In all the riots lasted four nights and when they ended the police reputation could hardly have stood lower.

In the public inquest which followed the police were attacked from all sides. Inevitably they were accused of being too rough and a two page advertisement appeared in the Socialist newspaper, *Het Vrije Volk*, accusing the police of indiscriminate arrests and maltreatment of suspects in custody. But even more significant was the official reaction. In the debate which followed in the Lower Chamber of the Netherlands Parliament, there was almost unanimous criticism of the police for their hesitant attitude. The Amsterdam correspondent of *The Times* expressed the official view in 'well informed quarters' in three succinct paragraphs:

When riots broke out on March 10, the day of the marriage, the police action was soft handed and since then rioting and disorder have been the order of the night.

It is considered that the press have given too much attention to the activities of the loafer, *provos* and even worse the Prime Minister lowered himself to having a one hour private talk with a *provo*. These loafers, going hand in hand with Communists and left wing socialists, have been for some time masters of the streets.

The prevailing opinion is that only by prohibiting street gatherings can order be restored to the city.[2]

Such a cry of despair clearly indicated that neither the Amsterdam authorities nor the Government had any idea of what had caused the riots or what to do about them. The authorities were driven back to notably false analysis such as 'soft handed' police action at the wedding and the only proposal put forward was to take more repressive action. The *Provos* had won their point and they had won it without being involved directly in the June riots.

The riots had been sparked off by the building workers and the young men and women who joined in were in the main on the fringe of the *Provo* movement. They were the young people who were ready to turn out for a happening, demonstration or riot alike. Many of the *Provos* stood aloof from the June riots and as one said afterwards: 'It was sad for us to see these youngsters following the methods of the strikers, throwing stones and breaking windows. We thought they might have learnt from us, have followed our pacifist ways. When we had trouble with the police we either sat down or walked away. We never shouted at them or harmed them.'[3] Yet the *Provos* could hardly complain. They had set the stage for the riots and the effect on their main target, the police, was profound.

After the riots Professor Heijder, Professor of Criminal Law and Criminal Policy at the University of Amsterdam, spent nine months working with the police on attachment. He says: 'After the riots the police did not know what to do or what to feel. They were quite unprepared and they had no attitude for what had happened. A policeman needs mental security above all else.' But this mental security was precisely what the police did not have. According to Heijder they did not understand what had happened and so put it down as either a revolutionary movement (and thus not police work) or the kind of incident which had happened before in Amsterdam. They refused to see it as innovative behaviour. 'Even today', says Heijder, 'many Amsterdam policemen define the *Provos* as political revolutionaries. They could not believe that there was not something behind it all.'

In retrospect the *Provos* may seem of only passing interest but this is to underestimate their influence. They are important for at least two reasons. First, 1966 showed unmistakably a sceptical younger generation who wanted to know *why*. They wanted to know why they were not allowed to dance in the streets and why they were not allowed to give raisins to passers-by. The fact that the policeman said it was not allowed was insufficient. The traditional police standard of 'my uniform is my authority' was not enough either for them or for the watching public. Second the *Provos* did succeed in showing something about the authorities. They set out to show how ridiculous the authorities would be when faced with situations they did not understand. They had succeeded in showing not only that but how repressive such auth-

46

orities could be when they were challenged – and that lesson did not go unnoticed. Two years later in Paris an attempt was made to provoke direct repression.

The starting point of the 1968 Paris revolution was the bleak university campus of Nanterre. Nanterre was built in the early 1960s to relieve the pressure on the Sorbonne. Several departments, including the Department of Sociology were farmed out to it. The contrast between Nanterre and the Sorbonne could hardly have been greater. The Sorbonne is set in the midst of the Latin Quarter with its wide boulevards, bustling pavement cafes and established student life: the Nanterre campus is positioned in a scruffy Paris suburb bounded on one side by tenement houses and on the other by the railway line into the centre of Paris. The French Ministry of Education in fact would have preferred another site but the pressure of sheer numbers on the French university system was so great that they went ahead with Nanterre rather than wasting time trying to find an alternative. Nanterre therefore was built as a direct response to numbers and it was these very numbers that helped to spark off the disturbances.

Under the French system of higher education, entry to university during the 1960s was easy enough but many students never finished their courses. The French preferred to do their weeding out after the students had begun rather than to impose more stringent entrance requirements. Such a system could hardly fail to produce instability and inside the student population it was a ready made and genuine source of grievance. Added to this there were other educational issues: at Nanterre and several other universities there was strong student feeling over the strict segregation of sexes into different residential blocks and restrictions on visiting rooms. But this was only part of the story. Nanterre also had its fair share of politically committed students. There was Daniel Cohn-Bendit whose philosophy went much wider than educational reform and aimed at challenging the whole capitalist system. There were members of the students union (UNEF) which had taken a strong political stand against the Algerian War and was now anxiously searching for a role. There were members of the various youth groups of the far left like the *Jeunesse Communiste Révolutionnaire* (JCR) many of whose members had been expelled by the Communist Party's own official youth movement. All these groups were then represented at Nanterre but they were a small minority. The story of the 1968 revolution is how this *'groupscule'* won not only the support of their fellow students but also the undoubted sympathy of the Paris population; of how they brought in the unions; and of how they came within an ace of toppling President De Gaulle himself. In all this the police played – or were made to play – a central role.

Once again the tactics of provocation were used but this time with even greater effect. The tactics of the leading theorists of the revolution like Cohn-Bendit clearly owed much to the example of the *Provos*. Cohn-Bendit's view was that the French capitalist system relied on the general apathy of the public to survive and was not as obliging as rotten systems had been in the past. 'Open physical repression with the point of a bayonet, as it was seen in the 19th Century, is now reserved strictly for the Third World.'[4] Traditional forms of protest like the peaceful demonstration had singularly failed to wake the public from this apathy. The need was for tactics which would provoke the authorities into revealing the bayonets which, according to Cohn-Bendit, had not been thrown away but simply kept out of sight in the capitalists' armoury. In fact it is doubtful whether these tactics were ever worked out quite so finely. Nor is it certain that even the analysis of Cohn-Bendit was necessarily correct. Christian Fouchet, who moved from the Department of Education to become Minister of the Interior in 1967 believed that the greatest mistake made was that the University authorities at Nanterre did not move quickly enough. As we shall see, Fouchet certainly made his own mistakes but in this first analysis he could well be right.[5] The early weakness and uncertainty of the university authorities at Nanterre helped the movement get off the ground. Faced with a campaign for university reform involving student strikes and a highly publicised incident when Cohn-Bendit berated the Government Minister of Sport who was opening a new swimming pool at Nanterre the university authorities did nothing. The view of the University Dean was that the heat would go out of the situation as the examinations approached. The view of Christian Fouchet was that the university authorities were allowing themselves to be terrorized by a small group of *enragés* (a term which goes back to the French Revolution and literally means wild one) and that things would only get worse.

It was Fouchet who was right and in March 1968 the real trouble began. On 18 March the windows of several American firms in Paris were blown in and two days later it was the turn of the American Express. The acts were directed against the Vietnam War and five members of left wing groups, one from Nanterre, were arrested. On 22 March a protest meeting was held at Nanterre; the Administrative Block was occupied and a manifesto issued by 142 of the students which protested at the arrests. The position now swiftly deteriorated. At the end of March lectures were suspended for a few days and during April preparations were made to boycott the examinations. Finally on Thursday, 2 May, three hundred *enragés* seized a lecture hall, excluded a history professor from his own lecture, and instead showed a film of the symbolic figure of revolution, Che Guevara. The same evening the Dean of Nanterre ordered the Faculty to be closed and six students (including the ubiquitous Cohn-Bendit) were ordered to appear on the following Monday at a disciplinary committee of the university in Paris. The explosion was fast approaching but on this same Thursday the Prime Minister, Pompidou, left on an official visit to Iran and Afghanistan.

The scene now changed to the paved courtyard of the Sorbonne. On the Monday, 6 May, five hundred students gathered to protest at the closure of Nanterre. In the main they represented the most politically committed among the student population and were still very much in the minority. They refused calls from university authorities to disperse and, according to the official account, began to make preparations for an attack which was rumoured to be on its way – but never came – from the right wing group Occident. It was undoubtedly a difficult situation but it was by no means out of control. But at this crucial point the decision was taken to call in the police to clear the courtyard. It was this decision which escalated a difficult demonstration into a bloody riot and which inevitably led to the violence of the following weeks.

Fouchet himself comments that the Sorbonne occupied a sensitive spot in the nerve system of the French nation. No Minister of the Interior any more wanted a confrontation with the students of the Sorbonne than a struggle with the miners or with the fishermen of Brittany. Nevertheless, the decision was quickly taken not only to tackle the students but to tackle them on their own territory – the courtyard of the Sorbonne flanked by the statues of Victor Hugo and Louis Pasteur. The original request for police intervention came from the Rector of the University and was passed on to Fouchet by Alain Peyrefitte, the Minister of Education. Neither Minister saw how they could refuse a written request from the Rector of the University and the order went out to Grimaud, the Prefect of the Paris police that he should clear the courtyard 'without violence and the minimum of force.'

Even with this decision taken it was just possible that the crisis could have been averted but the police not content with moving on the students decided 'quite naturally' (Fouchet's words) to carry out a quick identity check. There were after all rumours of the involvement of foreign students in the French protest. But the only way that such an identity check could be carried out was at the police station and the students were therefore bundled into police vans. Apparently Fouchet believes that even this could have gone off without incident had it not been for the false rumour which spread 'like a trail of powder through the quarter' that the students were being arrested and carted off to prison.

Yet on the face of it this would seem a highly predictable reaction. From the student vantage point all that could be seen was that colleagues were being arrested and then paraded as captives before their eyes. As Cohn-Bendit puts it 'emerging from their libraries, from their lectures or simply strolling back along the Latin Quarter students suddenly found themselves face to face with riot police blocking the gates of the Sorbonne.' As the first police van tight packed with students left there were jeers and shouts from the watching crowd. First stones were thrown and students pounded the sides of the police vans with their fists. The police responded with gas grenades and the subsequent riots lasted for almost twenty-four hours. For the first time the general student population was involved in the protest. The tactics of provocation had achieved a significant victory.

From the police point of view the turn of events was disastrous. The die had now been cast and they had been committed to a trial of strength with the students. The first riot had broken out and there was now little room for manoeuvre. The only result could be a battle between the *gardiens de la paix*, the CRS (*Compagnies Républicaines de Sécurité*) and the *Gendarmerie* on one side and the students on the other. Worst of all it was a battle for which the Paris public had not been prepared and had not had time to digest and consider the issues in debate. Almost inevitably then public sympathy lay with the young students: the obvious under-dogs.

As the riots continued public opinion swung even more sharply against the police. Slogans like 'A bas la répression' and the highly emotive 'SS:CRS' began appearing on walls. On 7 May when the students paraded through Paris the middle class applauded from their windows. Fouchet's secretariat was swamped with calls protesting about 'police brutality' and the Minister himself began to receive anonymous letters. Outside the capital it may be true that there was some feeling that the military should have been called in but in Paris itself the public were heavily on the side of the students. This support was carried to such an extent that on 8 May a public opinion poll was published which showed four fifths of Paris in favour of the students. However, the response from the Government was the same: there would be no negotiations before order had been restored. As De Gaulle put it: 'if order is restored then everything is possible.'

But order was not restored and the police were next faced with the night of the barricades. Fouchet's first reaction to UNEF's call for a massive demonstration on 10 May was to ban it: under French law any demonstration using the Paris streets has to be expressly authorized by the Prefect of Police. But Grimaud did not see how he could deploy his forces – which at no stage were more than twenty-six thousand – so that they would physically prevent the demonstration from taking place. Instead Grimaud tried to control the demonstration and positioned his forces around the perimeter of the Latin Quarter to prevent the demonstrators spilling over onto the right bank. Thus when the leaders of the demonstration which had assembled at the Place Denfert Rochereau and which was now about twenty thousand strong tried to cross the Seine on their way to the Headquarters of the French radio system they found their way blocked by police vans parked bumper to bumper. The students were pushed back on the area around the Sorbonne and were in effect imprisoned in a tight cordon. Their reaction, rather than try to break through was to stand and fight on the ground that they knew best. It was at this stage – between about 9.00 pm and 10.00 pm – that the first barricades of *pavés,* traffic signs and cars started going up.

Fouchet's view was that the police should have intervened im-mediately to prevent this but, as he is at pains to point out, it was the Prefect of Police who was responsible for the *'technique de l'ordre'*. To use his own analogy, the Minister of the Interior was the General in overall control: the Prefect of Police, the Commander on the ground making his own decisions based on the most up to date information. Grimaud's information was that negotiations were belatedly taking place between the students and the university authorities and he preferred to wait for the outcome. He did not have long to wait. Shortly after midnight Cohn-Bendit emerged from the negotiations with the words 'we told the Rector that what is happening in the streets tonight is a whole generation rising against a certain sort of society. We told him blood would flow if the police did not leave the Latin Quarter.' An hour after Cohn-Bendit's statement the police were sent in with orders to bring down the barricades.

For the next four hours a savage battle was waged. On one side were the police using gas grenades and all the modern paraphernalia of riot control. They seemed to represent overwhelming force. As one account puts it 'in this war game the sinister and terrifying police – masked, goggled, helmeted, clad in gleaming black from head to toe were cast in the role of evil spirits initiating the innocents to the cruelty and bestiality of the world.'[6] In fact, whatever the appearance, the true position was very different. Many students came prepared and hoping for battle. As one said afterwards:

> I went to the demonstration that evening, helmeted as usual and with a club which I hoped to be able to use, and then we went to the Science Faculty. There were quite a lot of us . . . and they were all very purposeful. There were far fewer slogans, very little was said, even amongst ourselves which was not the way it had been before. It was quite obvious that people wanted direct violent action.[7]

They were not disappointed.

By the time the night of the barricades came to an end four hundred people had been injured and two hundred cars either damaged or destroyed. Several hundred students had been arrested and worried parents besieged police stations and hospitals for news of the missing. Although there is no doubt that excessive violence was used on both sides it was the police who were almost exclusively the target for criticism. They were accused of attacking

Red Cross volunteers taking the wounded off stretchers and beating them further; and on one occasion they were charged with breaking into a flat and driving a girl naked into the streets. In the early hours of the morning of 11 May Fouchet was telephoned by a university professor who appealed to him to stop the 'butchery'. Fouchet replied 'who are you talking about? the young people who are injuring policemen with paving stones and building barricades in the middle of Paris, or the policemen who are trying to restore order?' The question was purely rhetorical. The public were talking about the police.

It was at precisely this point – when the police reputation could hardly have been at a lower point – that Prime Minister Pompidou at last returned from Afghanistan. A few hours later the whole policy was reversed. The Sorbonne was to be reopened and the Court of Appeal would give judgement on the imprisoned students. From the Government's point of view it was the only policy course open: from the police point of view it seemed like a complete disavowal of their role over the previous ten days. As the French Police Union said with considerable truth: 'We find it astonishing in these circumstances that a dialogue with the students was not started before these regrettable riots occurred.' The policemen felt that they had been made the sacrificial lambs for the change of policy and at one stage there seemed a real chance that there might even be a police strike.

Pompidou's action probably saved the situation but it did not have an immediate effect. On 13 May there was an immense demonstration, eight hundred thousand strong, through the centre of Paris in which for the first time the Unions and workers joined in. The Sorbonne was reopened and promptly occupied by the students and although De Gaulle left for Roumania a few days later, he was forced to return by the disturbances and disruption at home. By 22 May there were nine million on strike in France and two days later De Gaulle was forced to make a broadcast to the nation promising a referendum and national talks on pay. But even this was not enough and the violence continued. At Lyon a police inspector was killed and in Paris Pompidou was forced to give the police instructions to prevent further demonstrations. The result was that on 24 May Paris experienced probably its worst night of violence.

Cohn-Bendit believes that the night of the 24th could have spelt the end for De Gaulle. Whether he is right or not there is no doubt that France was as much saved from turmoil by the divisions of the left as by the action of the State. The Unions disliked and mistrusted the students and the students were divided among themselves about their tactics. Cohn-Bendit believes that the aim should have been to capture and occupy public buildings like the headquarters of the French broadcasting system but he comments scathingly that the 'revolutionaries' of UNEF and JCR were incapable of grasping the potential of the movement which had left them far behind. He believes that had Paris woken to find the most important Ministries occupied Gaullism would have caved in at once.

In this he may well have been right but as it was De Gaulle was allowed the time he so badly needed to recover and most of all to rally his own supporters. On Thursday, 30 May he made his crucial speech to the nation. The National Assembly was to be dissolved and new elections were to be held. France he said was threatened by Communist dictatorship and he appealed to the public to rally to the cause of the Republic. It was a powerful speech and it was immediately followed by an impressive pro-Gaullist demonstration through the centre of Paris. The counter Revolution had begun and the stage had been set for De Gaulle's crushing victory at the polls at the end of June.

Yet that victory should not disguise the fact that the authorities – Government, educational and police – had handled the whole affair with incredible ineptitude. Inaction was followed by over reaction and not until the very last stage did the authorities come to terms with the situation. Even when writing his memoirs three years later Fouchet insisted that the closest comparison with 1968 was the riots of 1934 in which the police opened fire and thirteen civilians were killed. He (rightly) takes pride in the fact that in spite of the level of violence there were very few deaths and that even on the night of the barricades the police did not use their firearms but Fouchet was unable to grasp the further lessons of 1968. He recognized the power of independent radio stations, like Radio Luxembourg (and bitterly complained of it) but the Government did precious little to win the public over to their side. Rather than giving the public time to make up its mind the police were committed to precipitate action. It was only at the eleventh hour that the Government appealed to the public – and even then they were saved as much by the divisions on the left as by the magic of De Gaulle.

In all this no one suffered more than the police. Their own casualties were heavy and throughout they were subject to bewildering changes of policy. The police were given the repressive tasks of clearing the Sorbonne and dismantling the barricades but immediately this had been completed they were apparently rejected by the Government who had been responsible for the orders. Yet when the first stage of Pompidou's conciliation policy failed they were again put back into action breaking up demonstrations and in the later stages expelling workers from factories. The police were used to extricate the State from its own mistakes and in so doing gathered for themselves a substantial legacy of distrust from a generation who in twenty years time will be leading France. For the theorists of the tactics of provocation the revolution represented practical success just falling short of total – but nevertheless exceeding their wildest dreams.

4

Europe Today

In most European nations today policemen are held in reserve to deal with demonstrations or riots. One of the best prepared of these forces is the *gendarmerie mobile* in France. Each squadron has a command vehicle with protected windows, radio and public address equipment; the coaches which carry the men are heavily protected and carry a store of tear gas. The *gendarmes* themselves wear helmets with visors to cover their faces; carry shields; and use their unloaded rifles as batons. Their jackets and trousers are fire proofed and padded; and so designed that there are no lapels or pockets where a demonstrator can take grip. In action their tactics are the tactics of deterrence. The men form into a line, give a low shout, and advance with the buses following behind with their sirens blaring. 'The aim', said a senior officer, 'is to dissuade by a show of strength.'

In other countries the precautions are very much the same. The Amsterdam police now have riot squads made up of the youngest (and fittest) policemen straight from police school. For four months they are trained in riot control and for the next thirty months act as a reserve which can be called from normal duties to deal with the emergency. Their equipment includes helmets, shields, and truncheons – together with tear gas and carbines. In Germany young policemen are also held on 'stand-by'. These are policemen under training at police schools who when operational come under the control of their instructors and can be sent into action in both a local or a national emergency; such as the protest in February 1977 over the siting of a nuclear power station near Hamburg when 6,500 policemen were deployed. The policemen are equipped with shields and helmets and among the supporting armaments are the armoured car and the water cannon. In Italy there are reserve forces stationed in barracks in cities like Rome, Naples, Milan, Turin, Florence and Bologna which can be called into action to deal with demonstrations. Again the men making up the squads are the youngest in the force and apart from the usual European riot control equipment bullet proof vests are on their way to becoming standard issue.

Yet for all this there are still policemen who believe that the technical measures should be even further strengthened. In Paris one policeman complained about the limitations of the water cannon. 'It is too immobile and difficult to manoeuvre', he said, 'If we were able to use coloured water to mark them it might be different. We have asked many times but so far the answer has always been "no".' In every European country there are policemen who take this kind of view. Their belief is that the vast majority of the public respect and obey the policeman simply because he is a policeman, and therefore all that is needed is better technical means of dealing with those who step over the line and challenge the policeman's authority. The view has an attractive simplicity – but it no longer prevails. The events of the late 1960s have persuaded the police policy makers – government ministers, civil servants and senior policemen – that the well equipped riot squad is only part of the answer. The reserve forces remain but only from necessity. The decision to fire tear gas or trundle the water cannon into position is regarded not as a sign of strength but as a dangerous sign that the police are unable to cope in any other way. The goal of practically every police administrator in the Common Market is a permanently better relationship between police and public and here Britain is seen as an example. As the press in Europe never cease to point out Britain has managed successfully without the elaborate equipment of crowd control. Newspapers still delight in reminding policemen in countries like France, Germany and Holland that in 1968 when most European capitals saw bitter street fighting London was able to escape serious trouble. The events of 1968 are therefore portrayed as a triumph for the British police and a corresponding failure on the part of most other forces. Yet just how fair is such a comparison?

There is no doubting that Britain faced a serious threat of violence in 1968. In March London had seen a demonstration which had developed into what one paper called 'Britain's worst political riot since the War'.[1] The occasion had been a ten thousand strong protest against the Vietnam War which had culminated in a march on the United States Embassy in Grosvenor Square. There the violent wing of the demonstrators had battled with the police who guarded the approach to the Embassy building. In the fighting 117 policemen and 47 demonstrators were injured and there were almost 250 arrests. By French and German standards this was comparatively small beer but it was enough to alarm (and indeed outrage) a public who had become accustomed to the peaceful protest of the Campaign for Nuclear Disarmament marches. Nor was this alarm allayed when the next day the police disclosed that searches of some of the coaches intercepted on the way to the demonstration had produced marbles and pebbles for use against police horses; imitation blood for the benefit of the television cameras; and even a number of unused .22 cartridges. The feeling of unease was completed when the then Home Secretary, James Callaghan, told the House of Commons that he was in no doubt that there was 'a great deal of international preparation behind these demonstrations.'

The next few months saw increasing speculation about the prospect of violence. There was a feeling that after Paris and Berlin it would next be the turn of London. Concern centred around the activities of the Vietnam Solidarity Committee which was a collection of left wing groups who had been responsible for the March demonstration and were planning a further protest in October. The fears about the October demonstration were suddenly crystalized by a dramatic (if exaggerated) front page story in *The Times* on 5 September which claimed that the demonstration would be used as an opportunity for militance. The story said:

A small army of militant extremists plans to seize control of certain highly sensitive installations and buildings in Central London next month while 6,000 Metropolitan policemen are busy controlling an estimated crowd of 100,000 anti-Vietnam war demonstrators on a peaceful march.

It added:

Police and leaders of the peaceful demonstrators share the view that 27th October could bring the most violent upheaval in Britain for many years. Some senior officials believe that they are faced with a situation potentially as violent as the student demonstrations in Paris and Berlin earlier this year.

From then onwards the advance press coverage of the demonstration was massive and even those newspapers who challenged the accuracy of *The Times* prediction did not doubt that there could easily be serious trouble on a scale not seen in London since the Fascist riots of the 1930s.

Yet from the very start of the demonstration it seemed unlikely that the worst predictions would be fulfilled. The first marchers started out shortly after 2.00 pm on Sunday afternoon, 27 October. They marched into Fleet Street in tight ranks under banners ranging from 'Save Biafra' to 'Free Greece'. In numbers they were certainly strong – although nowhere approaching the hundred thousand which the most optimistic organizers had expected – but they were well ordered and hardly seemed set on destruction. As they passed the newspaper offices there were cat-calls and the inevitable rhythmic chant of 'Ho, Ho, Ho Chi Minh' but the abuse was strictly verbal. From Fleet Street the main group made their way up Whitehall (where a petition was handed in at the Prime Minister's office in Downing Street) and eventually to the traditional home of London protest at Hyde Park. Here there were speeches including one from Tariq Ali (who had been built up as Britain's Cohn-Bendit) who told the crowd: 'This is not the end. This is the beginning of our campaign.' It was really no more than what a successful election candidate might tell his supporters after the declaration of the poll – and certainly it was a far cry from Cohn-Bendit's calls to action at the Sorbonne.

The mass of the demonstrators then simply went home and the only serious trouble was caused by a group of about six thousand who had detached themselves from the main march and made for the old target of the United States Embassy. In Grosvenor Square they found a waiting cordon of police and between 5.00 and 6.00 pm there were two concerted attempts to break through. Both were unsuccessful and although there were some fights (including one caught by a press photographer in which a policeman was held down while one demonstrator kicked him in the face) most again contented themselves with shouting abuse at the police as they drifted away. The challenge had been met and at surprisingly small cost. Four policemen and fifty demonstrators had been injured – most slightly – and forty-two arrests had been made. The night came to an end with demonstrators and policemen joining together in a chorus of 'Auld Lang Syne'.

When Mr Callaghan came to review the day at the Home Office he was quick to call it 'a demonstration of British good sense.' He added 'I doubt if this kind of demonstration could have taken place so peacefully in any other part of the world.' The same thought was echoed elsewhere. The next day an editorial in *The Guardian* commented 'The Metropolitan Police gave an example to the world in calmness and control.' A day later the American journalist, Karl E Meyer, wrote in *The Times*:

What did *not* happen, quite simply, was something that has occurred in every other major western country this year, a truly violent confrontation between angry students and sadistic police.

Yet most of the immediate comment missed one point: the tactics of provocation, as practised in Paris and Amsterdam, were not employed against the police in London. Rather than court a confrontation outside the United States Embassy the mass of the demonstrators marched perfectly peacefully to Hyde Park. Had they chosen to aim for Grosvenor Square then the outcome might have been very different. Looking back Tariq Ali now thinks the decision to go to Hyde Park was a mistake. According to his account the original plan was to march on Grosvenor Square (although some would have preferred to make for the Bank of England and others the South Vietnamese Embassy) but this was dropped after the newspaper predictions of violence.[2] Instead Hyde Park was agreed as a compromise and the decision was also taken that discipline would be maintained on the march and that only if the police interfered would the demonstrators fight back. Among the militants these decisions and subsequent lack of violence are blamed for what they saw as the failure of the demonstration. Yet even that analysis is open to question.

Had the leaders of the demonstration decided on a more violent course there is no certainty that they would have been followed. A survey carried out among the protesters themselves found that they were in no way as extreme as the advance publicity suggested.[3] It was true that most were opposed to the capitalist system but less than one quarter were protesting against all forms of authority. It was true that most supported the Vietcong but even so forty-two per cent would have settled for a compromise solution in Vietnam. It was true that seventy per cent expected there to be violence but – most significant of all – only ten per cent expected to be personally involved in it themselves. By British standards they still made up a difficult enough demonstration to handle and were certainly very different from the determinedly peaceful marchers of the Campaign for Nuclear Disarmament. Yet even so they were a long way from the ready armed students of Paris or the instant rioters of Amsterdam.

The fact is that in any demonstration it must be the demonstrators who largely call the tune. Since the war London has been fortunate: other cities like Paris noticeably less so. In Paris there are today small but significant groups who have spurned altogether moderate means and are prepared not only to advocate but to use violence. The *gauchistes* – a label which takes in extreme left wing groups like the Maoists and Trotskyites as well as anarchist groups – pose a continual threat. Five years after the October Revolution in 1973 two thousand *gauchistes* deliberately attacked the police who were protecting a meeting called to protest over the number of foreign workers in France. Molotov cocktails were thrown at the police and two ambulances taking an injured policeman and a civilian to hospital were surrounded and deliberately set on fire with the injured men still inside.

The Paris police then have to deal with a kind of demonstrator virtually unknown in Britain – although not in Ulster. One French policeman put the point:

> The aim of the *gauchistes* is to injure the police. If they can leave a policeman dead so much the better. Before 1968 the only organised group was the Communists. Now the *gauchistes* are very well organised. Their molotov cocktails are much more sophisticated than 1968 – the days of petrol in a milk bottle are over. Today they will do almost anything.

Nor is Paris alone. Amsterdam still sees riots of a kind rarely experienced in London. In March 1975, for example, a decision by the city authorities to pull down some old houses led to a riot in which the police were pelted with stones and even paving stones.[3] National traditions are also different. The London public has an undoubted affection for the Metropolitan Police. According to French policemen, 'Paris is a city of cop haters'; while most Dutch policemen agree that although respect for the police is high in the country districts of Holland 'you cannot say the same in Amsterdam.'

Worst of all is the position in Rome. According to a senior police official the antagonism is a hang-over from the years of Mussolini. 'We were then seen as part of the state apparatus. It will need many years to change that feeling.' Although many Italians trace back the origin of the public's dislike of the police much further there is general agreement that it will take a long time to overcome. In the meantime the police operate under difficulty and danger. On demonstrations their men wear bullet proof vests for the very good reason that they might be shot. In 1976 forty-six Italian policemen and carabinieri were killed; and in 1975 the death toll was forty-one. Most were killed by either terrorists or armed criminals but demonstrations also claim their casualties: such as the policeman shot dead during a police effort to end a student occupation at Rome University in April 1977. As one Italian policeman put it: 'Once they threw stones. Then they contented themselves with molotov cocktails. Now they use revolvers.'

Yet if the London demonstrators in 1968 behaved with moderation so too did the authorities and the police. In Paris the crucial decision had been the order to clear the courtyard of the Sorbonne. In London the equivalent decision was whether to allow the 27 October demonstration to take place and the Home Secretary was under strong pressure to ban it. Such a decision could well have been disastrous. The prohibition of a demonstration automatically places the authorities and the police in a repressive role. Their job becomes to prevent rather than to control. If only a small number of demonstrators decide to continue then a confrontation with the police becomes inevitable and that prohibition could reduce the demonstration to its militant hard core. It is a tactic of last resort and uncertain effect. In London the most probable result of prohibition would have been to have pushed the moderates into the arms of the militants and have made violence more, rather than less, likely.

So following Home Office tradition and advice Mr Callaghan allowed the demonstration to continue and relied on the police to control it. For their part the police were careful not to accentuate the division between themselves and the demonstrators. As the marchers wound their way to Hyde Park policemen marched with them flanking both sides of the procession. They were cheerful; they were unarmed; and they were clearly not to be easily provoked. At Grosvenor Square the police turned a blind eye to the minor skirmishing and stoicly bore the minor missiles which came their way. According to one observer 'for the first time in history a massed police force practised passive resistance.'[4] Nevertheless, for all their skill it would be a profound mistake to believe that tactics alone explained the police success. Such tactics were only possible because of the broad acceptance and support given to the police by the public. Most demonstrators accepted the police presence: there was a *rapport* between police and protesting public. The British authorities were able to plan on the basis that this was likely to be so but in other European cities no similar assumption could be made. The students of Paris would no more accept the CRS than the *Provos* would accept the policemen of Amsterdam.

The October 1968 demonstration in London showed that the British acceptance of their police is still a considerable buffer against convulsion. It enables any Government more easily to follow a course of moderation. It acts as an instinctive check on all but the most militant and implacable protesters. And it helps the policemen themselves to do without the para-military paraphernalia of crowd control like the water cannon and the tear gas cannister. If London holds a lesson it is the dominating importance of good relations between police and public – and it is this lesson that Europe has taken most closely to heart.

In Britain the relationship between police and public has been able to develop undisturbed. The British police has never been seen as the instrument of a repressive government; the country has never been occupied; and there have been no seizures of power. Over the years the public have come to trust and admire the police and it has never proved necessary to run an explicit 'support your police' campaign. In other Common Market countries the history has been very different and the difficulties correspondingly greater. The basis of the public's support for the police has been more unsure and the result has been that throughout the Seventies European governments have tried a variety of methods to win over the public – including direct advertising. In Paris there have been advertising campaigns in newspapers and *Metro* stations under the slogan *Merci, Monsieur L'Agent*. While in Germany and Holland similar campaigns have been run to establish the police as the 'public's friend'. A further sign of the police concern has been the formation of psychological sections in police forces in both Germany and Holland.

The first psychological section was formed in Munich in 1964 when in the aftermath of student unrest in the city a consultant psychologist was hired to examine ways in which relations between police and public could be improved. Since then the section has expanded and regular policemen work together with a professional psychologist directly advising the president of police. They help in the instruction of policemen including not only recruits but also middle and senior ranks. They visit schools to explain the police role – 'the school pupil of today is the student of tomorrow and the demonstrator the day after that' – and they advise on man management inside the service. In demonstrations they act as a kind of go-between advising the police on tactics. Munich's example has now been followed by most German police forces. The result is that a force like that of Bremen today employs two fully trained psychologists who both teach and advise the police on tactics.

At Bremen every course held at the police school, housed in a barracks on the outskirts of the city, includes psychology. According to staff there the instruction is of help to both new recruits and the older policeman. One staff member said:

The aim is quite simply to help the policeman with his work – how to approach people, how to cope with a stress situation. We try to make him understand the changing nature of police work. The older man in particular tends to think in terms of authority and that authority is automatically given to him by the uniform he wears. That used to be enough but it certainly is not enough today. The public want to know why. If a policeman tells a man to do something he is likely to turn round and say – 'why the hell should I?' We have a critical public and we have to try and train our men so that they are capable of dealing with that critical public.

Bremen also provides a good example of the change of tactics which has resulted. In 1968 students at the local university protested at increases in fares by sitting on the tram rails. The police were sent in with orders to move them and the result (not surprisingly) was a pitched battle between police and students. Nine years later in 1977 the same situation arose after a further increase in fares. This time the police allowed the students to sit where they were and diverted the trams onto other routes. The protest certainly took longer to overcome but the public's anger centred on the students not the police. As one policeman said:

> In 1968 quite a lot of the public sympathised with the students and accused the police of brutality. This time there were some who said we should have been tougher but in the main the shop assistant who now had to walk some way to get on the new tram route criticised the demonstrators. There were one or two cases when we had to protect the students from the public.

Not surprisingly support for the introduction of psychologists has its critics among German policemen. Some reckon they are good at advising on what went wrong after the event; while a different criticism is that it would be better to send policemen to train as psychologists rather than introduce psychologists to police work. ('He doesn't know the problems of the man sitting in the patrol car or the difficulties of a man patrolling a down town problem area'). Nevertheless most German policemen reckon that the psychologist is there to stay. In Amsterdam the police also introduced a psychologist when they were still reeling from the *Provos'* assault. The first psychologist was given a fairly rough ride by the city's policemen and was basically confined to working at the police school. His successor, however, was much more accepted and attended the weekly meetings of the senior police officers basically to advise on tactics and to interpret the public to the police. As one senior policeman put it: 'The police are an "in" group. The psychologist is there to put the outsider's point of view.'

The Italian police have not yet formed psychological sections but other fundamental changes are promised. When the police was re-established after the Second World War it remained a semi-military body – more comparable to the *carabinieri* than a civil police force. In the last ten years the defects in this arrangement have become more and more obvious. From the outside the police have been attacked for violence and accused of indiscriminate shooting in emergencies.

From the inside policemen have protested at the repressive role they have been given and have campaigned for police reform. The reform movement started in the Autumn of 1969 when the police found themselves being used to break up demonstrations by workers demanding pay increases and better conditions – demands which the police themselves supported. This was followed by years of serious police unrest including a case in 1976 when a young police captain was put on trial after he claimed that men in the mobile squads were 'sick of making violence a way of life' and accused policemen of acting as *agents provocateurs* in demonstrations. The symbol of this new movement has been the demand of policemen to have union representation (on the lines of the Police Federation) which for years was resisted on the grounds that the police were a disciplined body. Today, however, the Italian Government accept the case for reform and the formation of a police union is only a matter of time.

The activities of the demonstrators and rioters then have concentrated wonderfully the minds of most police forces in West Europe. The importance of maintaining good relations between police and public is now seen as the first aim of policy and the British position is often regarded as the goal. Yet Britain herself would be very unwise to rest on her laurels. When the Royal Commission on the Police reported in 1962 they published a survey of public opinion which showed that eighty-three per cent of the public professed great respect for the police; sixteen per cent said they had mixed feelings; and only one per cent said they had little or no respect for them. The Royal Commission commented: 'We therefore assert confidently that relations between the police and the public are on the whole very good.'[5] In 1969 another opinion poll showed that ninety-five per cent of the public believed the British police to be honest and helpful; and ninety-three per cent thought them friendly and fair.[6] A further survey in 1973 showed them as the most respected occupational group in Britain with seventy per cent of the public reporting 'a great deal of confidence in the people running the police.'[7] While a National Opinion Poll in London in 1974 showed that policemen were considered the most important group serving the community.

Yet too much should not be made of these findings. A survey carried out in Germany after the 1968 student riots showed that even then sixty-five per cent of the German public had complete faith in the police; twenty-five per cent gave qualified approval; and only seven per cent had no faith in the police.[8] Since then the wider recognition of the terrorist threat has strengthened public support. While in France a poll commissioned by five major provincial newspapers showed that seventy-four per cent of the

French public viewed the police with sympathy and only fourteen per cent with hostility.[9] Certainly the British results are generally better – particularly among young people where the French police score badly – but the French police are, after all, reckoned to be one of the most unpopular forces in Western Europe. Nor, of course, can any British police administrator fail to be concerned by the most recent developments in relations between police and public. The battles between political extremists in 1977 at Lewisham and Ladywood and the violence of industrial disputes like Grunwick have resulted in both physical and verbal attacks on the police.

For the police in any country the wisest view is to treat the generalized findings of opinion polls with the caution of politicians and to accept that even the most comforting picture can change quickly and radically. No government can afford to take support for the police for granted – particularly in a period of economic crisis and constitutional debate – and re-examination of policies should be a continual process. No police force can afford to forget that they are now dealing with a better educated, better informed and more sceptical public. Police policy in a democracy must recognize this. As Professor Heijder said in Holland 'You can only use exclusively police methods in a police state. Here it is impossible. They all go to the European Commission on Human Rights – and rightly so.' In the democracies of Europe the policeman must earn the public's respect. It is no longer enough to say 'my uniform is my authority.' At the same time governments must keep the respect and support of the policemen upon whom they rely.

5

The Big, The Small, and The National

Nothing so divides policemen as the debate on how they should be organized. In Britain the debate has raged since the inception of the police itself and the frustration of the earliest plans for a national force. In other European countries proposals for change have also been fiercely resisted and in the Netherlands the opposition has been so successful that the Dutch police seem to be forever frozen in a nineteenth-century mould. The case for bigger forces can be simply put. It is that they avoid wasteful duplication of headquarters and services, provide a direct chain of command from the top, and offer advantages to policemen like better promotion prospects. The theory is that they are more efficient and therefore more likely to command public respect. The case against is much shorter. It is basically that forces can be too big and that this point arrives when the public fails to identify the force as *their* police. The policeman, it is argued, must be regarded as belonging to the area he serves rather than under the direction of some remote outside body. It is a debate then which is central to any discussion of relations between police and public, and Europe – where there are examples of police organization ranging from the large national structure down to the tiniest community force – provides a good check of the rival theories.

The Big
West Germany can fairly claim to have been the test bed of Europe. The immediate post war years saw the German police working under a unique variety of difficulties and dangers. Many of the new policemen had neither previous experience nor training and were recruited from the prisoner of war camps set up to take the defeated German armies. In Bavaria they were sent out on

duty armed with no more than staves at a time when men were being killed for their petrol coupons. Police murders were common and in several cases policemen were shot as they tried to arrest men stealing potatoes from the fields. In Bremen the American occupation forces saw the dangers and allowed the police to keep the arms of the men they arrested: a similar arrangement allowed the police to equip their offices. In the Ruhr the British treated the new police with extreme caution and insisted that they observe curfews in the same way as the public. Police policy was laid down by the Allied High Commission and could be summed up as de-militarization, de-Nazification, and above all decentralization. De-militarization was achieved by limiting arms and abolishing military ranks. De-Nazification was substantially achieved by weeding out the most obvious Nazis and recruiting men who were too young to have played any real part in Hitler's rise to power. But de-centralization proved much more difficult.

The theory was that once the police was broken down into a multitude of local forces this would automatically prevent the re-establishment of a state within a state. The policy as laid down by the High Commission was that de-centralization should go beyond the state (*Länd*) level and that independent community forces should be encouraged. This policy was most enthusiastically followed in the American zone of occupation where police forces were authorized in any community which had a population over five thousand. The British, who occupied much of the old state of Prussia and inherited the Prussian's centralized police tradition, did not go quite to the American lengths. They broke down the police into forty separate forces based roughly on cities with a population of over one hundred thousand. Only the French stood out against this trend. No attempt was made to break down the police below the state level and three state police forces were created controlled by the state government. In the event it was the French model which proved most lasting.

Within a few years of the end of the war the local forces were under attack. The argument used was that small local forces were all very well in an utopian world but when there was trouble the need was for a strong force and central control. In 1950 this argument was implicitly accepted by the High Commission when new instructions were issued allowing forces to be centralized at the state level. It is true that independent municipalities were allowed to maintain their own forces but even this right was limited. General regulations on police recruiting, training and promotion became the prerogative of the state and in an emergency the state took over the direction of all forces. The state Minister of the Interior was rapidly regaining his power and over the last twenty-five years this process has continued. By 1975 even the large municipal forces like Munich had disappeared. Police forces are now based on West Germany's eight constituent states together with the forces belonging to the city states of Berlin, Bremen and Hamburg.

Yet different as this structure may be from the plans of Germany's first post war administrators it is still a considerable way from a centralized national police. Power rests with the states and federal organizations are few. There is a national criminal investigation office (*Bundeskriminalamt*) at Wiesbaden but their job is to help the state detective forces rather than to replace them. The only force of any size controlled directly by the Federal Minister of the Interior in Bonn is the twenty thousand strong Federal Border Guard (*Bundesgrenzschutz*) which was formed in 1951 to control the politically sensitive national borders at a stage before the German army was re-armed. The border guard has jurisdiction in the thirty kilometres behind the border but its area of operations has now been extended to airports and even guarding embassies. Yet even on the border federal power is not complete and Bavaria is still allowed its own border guard – who were first with the news of Russia's invasion of Czechoslovakia.

In Germany then the trend has been unmistakably away from the small and even medium sized local forces to larger regional forces. A similar, although by no means as pronounced, movement has taken place in Britain. At the very time when the British were laying down one hundred thousand as the minimum population for police forces in Germany, many of their own forces did not meet this criterion. In 1945 over a third of the police forces in England and Wales had strengths of under one hundred and (the story goes) some chief constables took their turn in making the tea and manning the telephone. As late as 1962, when the Royal Commission on the Police reported there were still thirty-four police forces with population areas of under one hundred thousand including seven in the County of Lancashire alone. The Royal Commission set out to change all that and laid down five hundred or more as the optimum size of a police force: the equivalent of a population size of 250,000. Four years later the Labour Government put through an amalgamation programme which reduced the number of forces to forty-six, abolishing altogether the small municipal forces and compulsorily marrying together city and county forces like Nottingham and Nottinghamshire. Today there are forty-three forces in England and Wales including not only the traditional giant of the Metropolitan Police with a strength of over twenty-one thousand but other major forces like Lancashire and the West Midlands. The only small local force to have escaped the axe is the eight hundred strong force belonging to the City of London who have now successfully seen off Home Secretaries from Pitt to Roy Jenkins. In Scotland there are a further eight including the 6,500 strong Strathclyde force.

Significantly not even a Labour government has seriously considered introducing a national force. On the 1962 Royal Commission there had been support for a national force notably from the distinguished Oxford lawyer Professor A. L. Goodhart. Goodhart argued for a national force covering England and Wales controlled by the Home Secretary but administered by up to fifteen regional commissioners: a plan which would give more effective power to the Home Secretary than the French Minister of the Interior. In support he quoted the view of the constitutional authority Sir Ivor Jennings:

It is only by historical accident that the control of the police is vested in local authorities. Clearly the preservation of order is the fundamental duty . . . of any state. According to the principles of public administration the police should be under the control of central government.

Yet against the principles of public administration or not, the majority on the commission favoured continuing with a system which most witnesses had regarded as 'basically sound'. The theorists were defeated and both Royal Commission and Government placed its faith in the opinion of most (though not all) serving policemen.

Executive power then remains – where it has always been – in the hands of local chief constables. The Home Secretary can guide policy by issuing advice and he can check on efficiency by the reports of his inspectors. But he cannot control. In effect the chief constable is very much his own boss. He answers to a local police committee made up of magistrates and councillors – except in London where the Home Secretary is the police authority for the Metropolitan Police – but neither the police committee nor the Home Secretary has any operational role. Clearly, as in the case of violent demonstrations or picketing, there are consultations between the chief constables and the Home Secretary but this relationship is a long way from the German situation where the State Minister of the Interior will take command and has a police radio permanently in his car. In Britain the emphasis is on guiding the police rather than controlling it centrally. In the extreme a police committee can dismiss a chief constable and a Home Secretary could ultimately have his way by withdrawing the fifty per cent Government grant to all forces. But essentially the chief constable answers not to government but to the law.

The position then in Britain is that although forces are now appreciably bigger they remain independent. National organizations like the German border guard are unknown. Local jealousies between forces remain but the disappearance of the smallest also seems to have removed the most uncooperative. Traditionally the Metropolitan Police has provided assistance to local forces. Scotland Yard has acted as the headquarters of the national criminal record office and has also provided operational assistance outside London, particularly by specialist criminal investigation units like the murder squad. With the formation of the regional crime squads in the mid-Sixties, who like the French concentrate on serious crime, provincial England is now much more self-sufficient. Characteristically even the regional crime squads are controlled by committees of the local chief constables within each region.

The small

One advantage claimed for big police forces is the ability to respond to an emergency. In Holland the lack of effective machinery to deal with a crisis is one of the main arguments used by those who want to change the structure of the Dutch police. At present Holland is able to boast some one hundred and thirty local forces as well as a state police force under the Minister of Justice – which operates in the smallest towns and villages, all to police a population of about thirteen million. The state force is seven thousand five hundred strong and the local forces total around fifteen thousand ranging from Amsterdam and Rotterdam who are around the two thousand mark to the eighteen strong force in Harlingen, Friesland, which basically looks after a busy harbour. Such an organization might conceivably work if co-operation between forces was good but it is not and, as one policeman put it, 'the walls between forces are high.' Authority over the local forces rests (except for crime investigation) with the burgomasters and requests for help from other forces can be, and are, ignored. According to one city policeman 'everyone says it can't be done.'

Yet this is only one of the defects of the Dutch police structure. Over ninety forces have a strength of under one hundred which prevents adequate specialization and means that promotion opportunities are limited to dead men's shoes. Such defects then are obvious and, indeed, well recognized in Holland itself but agreement on the way forward has so far proved impossible – mainly because of the precarious parliamentary majorities of successive Dutch governments. One solution is for a national force but this is opposed not only by the small forces but the powerful city authorities as well. Another proposal is for about twenty-five local forces but this is opposed by the Ministry of Justice and the State Police who see their role substantially reduced. The problem is not a new one in Europe – and Holland is not the only European country which has failed to solve it.

In Belgium each of the country's *communes* is allowed to run its own urban police force which answers to the local mayor or *bourgmestre*. The result is a plethora of small forces – there are nineteen separate forces in the Brussels area alone, and all told about two hundred local forces throughout Belgium. In addition there are two national forces. The first is the judicial police (*police judiciaire*) who work solely on investigating crime and whose work is directed and co-ordinated by a central office in Brussels. While the second is the *gendarmerie* – which although constitutionally a military force coming under the direction of the Minister of Defence – also carries out a normal police role when it comes under the direction of either the Minister of the Interior or the Minister of Justice. Basically the *gendarmerie* polices the country areas – including the roads – but it can also work inside cities and towns. Among its units are mobile groups which can be used in an emergency.

The National

France is not the only European country with a national force but it certainly has the biggest. All told there are now almost two hundred thousand police for France's population of fifty-three million. Yet nationalization – which was pushed through by De Gaulle in 1966 – has not provided the French with a truly unified service. Responsibility is still divided between two government departments. The Ministry of the Interior has overall responsibility for the civil police which operates in Paris and in the big cities and towns; the Ministry of Defence controls the *Gendarmerie Nationale* which basically acts as the police force in the small towns with populations under ten thousand and the villages. Feelings between the two services are not always good. The police tend to regard the *gendarmes* as outdated and bitterly complain that, as the Ministry of Defence always receives a generous budget, it is able to lavish more money on the *gendarmerie* than ever comes the way of the police. In contrast the *gendarmes* take pride in their eight hundred year tradition and regard with some distaste police formations like the CRS whom they see not so much as violent but ill disciplined – the cardinal sin in the eyes of any self-respecting *gendarme*.

Inside the civil police (*la police nationale*) the new national structure has provided its problems. Command is exercised by the Minister of the Interior's chief executive, the director general of police whose headquarters in the Place Beauveau are connected with the Ministry and only a stone's throw from the Elysée Palace. The Director General now outranks even the Prefect of Police in Paris who had previously occupied a very special position in the French police system reporting directly to the Minister. Even today the Paris police maintain bravely 'we have one chief and that is the Prefect', but the fact is that the Prefect's position has been downgraded. His force is now smaller following the reorganization of boundaries and his direct line to the Minister has been interrupted. It is true that the Prefect of Police retains day to day control of the Paris police, but in an emergency he would now work in consultation with the Director General. The effect of the changes has been to bring the Paris police much more in line with practice outside the capital. Throughout France there are about four hundred and sixty permanent forces policing the big cities and towns with day to day control exercised by the mayor. However, in an emergency it is the prefect for the department – in effect the government's representative in the region – who takes over and in the most serious cases it is the prefect who would request the help of the CRS.

The *Compagnies Républicaines de Sécurité* is by far the most significant force which comes under the direct control of the Minister of the Interior. With the CRS there is not the same need to make separate arrangements for day to day control and control during emergencies. The emergency is the force's *raison d'être*. They are deployed at ten strategic points throughout France ready to deal with anything from a political demonstration to a workers' occupation of a factory. Each regional commander answers directly to the central command in the Ministry of the Interior in Paris and before they can be used the Minister must give his personal authorization. In essence then the CRS, which numbers about sixteen thousand officers and men is a reserve force which can only be activated by the Minister. It is only when they are activated that they fall under police control for the very good operational reason that it would be impossible to have a force acting independently. For the police this arrangement also has another considerable advantage. As one senior policeman put it: 'The local policeman lives there among the people. He has to stay after the emergency is over. The CRS is different. They come from outside and want to finish the emergency quickly.'

The criminal investigation side of the police – the *police judiciaire* – not only provides a separate career but is also divided on the basis of responsibility. At the national level there are detectives who can operate throughout France – mainly in the areas of drugs and counterfeit money – as well as a national criminal bureau which collects and provides information and intelligence. At the regional level there are seventeen regional crime squads formed in 1907 by Clemenceau – almost sixty years before Britain hit on the idea – to concentrate on serious crime requiring long and probably difficult investigation. While at the local level are the detectives who carry out the routine investigations in the cities and towns.

To this civil police strength should be added the seventy thousand strong *gendarmerie*. The command structure is a prime example of divide and rule. At the very top is the Minister for the Army; the director of the *gendarmerie* is a high ranking magistrate who will probably go on to become a judge; and the director's two deputies are both generals. The constitutional argument for the civilian director is that it prevents the *gendarmerie* becoming a private ministerial force but it also recognizes the fundamental dual role of the *gendarme*. The *gendarme* is a soldier with a civil role: a man who is trained both to fight and to investigate crime and control traffic. His most obvious appearance is as country policeman but his other jobs have a more military flavour. The *Garde Républicaine* is a specialist regiment stationed in Paris for the kind of ceremonial work carried out in London by the Brigade of Guards; while the *gendarmerie mobile* is a reserve force housed in barracks throughout France.

The men of the *gendarmerie mobile* work monthly shifts. The first month is spent as public order reserves; the second as reinforcement for the departmental *gendarmerie;* the third as a military stand-by which can only be activated by the Prime Minister; and the fourth month on a range of general duties like the transfer of prisoners. Their first task, however, is to maintain order and in a crisis this takes precedence over all else. The *gendarmerie mobile* then comes under civilian authority. Thus in Paris the Prefect of Police would ask the regional commander – a three star general based at Les Invalides – for help. Normally the general would refer the request to the Defence Ministry and bargaining would go on between the Ministry of Defence and the Ministry of the Interior on the exact numbers to be sent. Once a number is agreed then the Prefect of Police gives the *gendarmerie* their task although the *gendarmes* retain discretion on exact dispositions. Thus during the June 1973 riots in Paris the Prefect asked for a light squadron of lorries and jeeps. The *gendarmerie* replied that such a squadron was no use for the narrow streets to which it had been assigned and as a result was later used in the much wider Boulevard St Michel and Boulevard St Germain.

The only other Common Market nation of comparable size with a nationally organized police system is Italy – although responsibilities are so divided that the main effect somehow seems to be a bewildering range of national forces rather than a bewildering range of local forces. The *Guardia di Pubblica Sicurezza* (usually known as PS) comes under the control of the Minister of the Interior and, rather on the French lines, responsibility is passed down to a prefect representing the national government in each of Italy's ninety-five provinces. In each province a chief of police (*Questore*) reports to the prefect for normal everyday police work. However, when it comes to criminal investigation the structure is rather different. A new national co-ordinating body (*Criminalpol*) has been established in two office buildings in the garden suburb of Rome and further provincial offices have been established in Milan, Naples, Palermo and Cagliari. In the main the role of *Criminalpol* is to gather and send out information to the local forces – a national criminal index for example is kept in Rome – but they also have an investigating role in major crime. But this is not the only specialist force inside the national police. Among other forces (with distinctive uniforms) are frontier police for policing airports, ports and border posts; a railway police; and a traffic police. Responsibility however remains with the Ministry of the Interior and the police who staff the specialist forces have all undertaken the standard police training.

When it comes to the *Carabinieri* the position is fundamentally different. Like the *Gendarmerie* in France they come under the control of the Minister of Defence and also like the *Gendarmerie* they frequently command more public respect. Discipline is unmistakably military and the force take pride in a history which stretches back to 1814 when they were formed to preserve order in the Kingdom of Savoy. Yet not even this is a full total of the police forces in Italy. The *Guardia di Finanza* is a force under the control of the Treasury which combats crimes like smuggling, illegal entry and tax evasion; while at the local level there are municipal policemen (*Vigili Urbani*) who carry out work like the direction of traffic in the cities.

The other countries of the Common Market also have national police organizations of one kind or another but as their populations are small this is hardly surprising. The total of the police in Denmark, for example, is only eight thousand five hundred – less than half the strength of the Metropolitan Police in London. Command is in the hands of a National Commissioner of Police (*Rigspolitichefen*) who answers to the Minister of Justice. Even so the police is then broken down into fifty-five local forces of which the most important is Copenhagen with a strength of almost three thousand. Copenhagen has its own commissioner – the others have chief constables – and within the organization is an emergency force ready to deal with anything from a royal visit to a demonstration. The Danish police also provide men to police the forty thousand population of Greenland – where alcoholism remains one of the major problems and banishment survives as a possible punishment – while their role extends to administering driving tests and carrying out public health inspections. In Eire the national force followed the Anglo-Irish Treaty of 1921. Up until that time the Royal Irish Constabulary had policed all Ireland but following the treaty the Royal Ulster Constabulary was established in the north while the Garda Siochana was formed to police the twenty-six counties of the south. The Garda is centrally controlled and administered and comes under the command of a Commissioner who is responsible to the Minister of Justice in Dublin. In the Common Market's smallest country Luxembourg there are two national forces to police a population of about 320,000. The *gendarmerie* polices the country areas as well as the highways, railways and airport; while the police look after the towns. The only major peculiarity about the forces is that both are subject to military discipline and both are the responsibility of the Minister of the Armed Forces – although when operational they answer to either the Minister for the Interior or the Justice Minister.

What then does Europe contribute to the debate on the size of forces? There is an undeniable trend to larger forces and one fear among policemen is that this will automatically mean that they lose touch with the public. In the small Bavarian town of Miesbach nestling below the German Alps, one policeman echoed the views of many others throughout Europe when he said: 'Relations with the public have deteriorated. In the old days the policeman was on foot or on bicycle. He was talking directly with the farmers. Now he is always in a car and his only contact is when he wants to settle a dispute. Things would be better if you were able to get the policeman back on the beat or if he had more time. As it stands at the moment he is charging from one emergency to the next.'

Yet when it comes to it the public do want their emergencies dealt with first. This, of course, is the difficulty. The public want the best of both worlds. They feel quite genuinely that they want more men on the beat, but they also demand that the police organization is capable of meeting any emergency whether it be a demonstration, an outbreak of muggings or a terrorist attack. The police then must reconcile these twin – and often contradictory – demands as best they can.

Some policemen argue that no such balance is possible and that bigger forces must by definition mean a poorer local service. Ironically it is the centrally controlled *gendarmerie* in France who establish that this need not be the case. It is ironical because by most standards the *gendarmerie* appears as an anachronism among the civil police forces of Europe. Their tradition, discipline and attitude is unmistakably military. They aim for respect but no one can accuse them of courting easy popularity. As one officer put it: 'We were not created to be loved.' Even when investigating crime, they do so in uniform. This may all seem very unfashionable but the fact remains that they are accepted by the French public and that while both police and army find it difficult to attract enough recruits the *gendarmerie* turns men away.

As a police force their success comes from the way in which the organization is broken down to the small *brigades* of between five and thirty men who are the basic unit in the country areas. There the *gendarmes* and their families live in flats in the same building as the station office. There is a separate entrance for families but when off duty the *gendarme* must say where he can be contacted. The only exception to this rule is his weekly thirty-six hour rest period and his forty-five days annual leave. The result is that the *gendarmerie* can provide a twenty-four hour service and it is here that part of their strength lies. The other part is their commitment to and knowledge of the area they police. Some *gendarmes* have spent most of their service in the same area – which is often their home territory in any event – and the policy now is to avoid unnecessary moves. They occupy a position of respect in the local community and when they retire as often as not they remain in the same area. It would, of course, be absurd to believe that this model could be exactly duplicated elsewhere. For one thing few policemen outside the *gendarmerie* would contemplate a life spent living on top of the station and on constant call. Yet the point remains that even the biggest organization can be broken down and that national policemen can still be local.

The other main argument used against the bigger force, in particular the national force, is that it could become the tool of a would be dictator. This argument is neither historically convincing nor constitutionally valid. Hitler did not come to power on the back of a national police force: the national force was created only after he had seized power. As the 1962 Royal Commission remarked 'if any ill-disposed government were to come into office it would without doubt seize control of the police *however* they might be organized.' The constitutional argument against a national force is no more valid and rests on the basic misconception that liberty depends upon a particular form of police organization. The true position is that public freedom can only be safe-guarded if the police are subject to the law and accountable to the democratically elected parliament. In terms of potential revolution the greater danger to be faced today is that local forces may be too weak and thus unable to take effective action to counter any threat.

Of course this does not automatically make the case for a national force. The increasing demands made of the police in all their areas of operation mean that the small force of a few hundred has been outdated. It is unable to cope with the public's emergencies and therefore is in constant risk of falling into public contempt. Yet there is still a real choice between the centrally controlled forces of France; the large – but locally controlled – regional forces of Germany; and the big autonomous forces of Britain. Holland and Belgium will eventually have to choose between these models and it seems unlikely that in Britain – where most forces are still under 2,500 in strength – the debate has ended. The purists will again argue for national control on the grounds that as Ivor Jennings put it, local control is an 'historical accident'. Yet as historical accident explains so much about the police it seems folly to ignore it in this respect – especially when the last test of police opinion showed only six per cent in favour of a national force. While perhaps the conclusive argument for separate rather than national forces is that they enable chief constables to go ahead with new ideas without the need to await a Government decision. British police history is rich with examples of enterprising chief constables who have pushed ahead on their own – two of the most recent being Sir Eric St Johnstone who introduced the unit beat system in Lancashire, and of course Sir Robert Mark, who introduced one change after another at Scotland Yard.

On the other hand there is no reason why there should not be a further development of the concept of regional specialist squads supplementing the work of local forces. This idea was first tried out in Britain in 1963 and two years later the first nine regional crime squads were formed. (The French parentage of the regional squad was either unknown or went unacknowledged). The squads were given the task of concentrating on serious crime and crimes that clearly involved more than one force. Detectives were seconded from the local forces and as far as possible they were kept free of routine work. Implicitly the scheme recognized that times had changed: that crime was no longer just local: and that new forms of organization were needed to meet the challenge of the increasing number of criminals who moved around the country. It was a sensible advance and the clear potential exists for it to be extended further – so that, for example, drug offences and fraud are dealt with entirely regionally as well as perhaps the policing of motorways. Such changes would leave the local forces untouched but would hive off some of the more specialist functions. It would be a compromise which would seek to distinguish between those police functions where greater centralization would help and those where there was no obvious advantage in change.

In the debate on organization Europe established this. It is a myth that the local force automatically commands more public respect. This is certainly not the case in Holland or Belgium. Equally it is a myth that a national force – which all too easily can develop layers of bureaucracy – is necessarily more efficient. The French system is not noticeably more effective than either the German or the British. What is important is that whatever the organization it should then be broken down to enable the policeman to serve the local community. In the country areas and the towns this is not too difficult. In the cities – whether it be London, Paris or Munich – it is an infinitely harder task.

Europe raises one further question: the place of the reserve force. Periodically it is argued that Britain would be well advised to have a national reserve force which could be called in in case of emergency and certainly it is true that most European countries now have such reserves. France probably has the strongest reserve strength with the CRS and the *gendarmerie mobile* but Italy also holds substantial reserves. On paper West Germany would appear to have strong reserve forces with both the 'stand-by' police and the border police – although some German policemen would argue that it would be difficult to activate the reserve quickly in case of a sudden emergency. While even the smaller nations of Europe – like Belgium – can also call in an emergency force. In contrast the major reserve force in Britain is the Special Constabulary: a force of civilian volunteers who help out on routine duties in their spare time and which in concept is light miles away from the CRS and the like. Nevertheless it would be a profound mistake to regard the formation of a professional reserve as a sign of strength.

No government from choice would have hundreds of men more or less permanently held in reserve when the need for policemen on general duties is so acute. Reserve forces can only be justified when the threat of emergency is continual. In Paris and Rome there is no question that such a threat exists with frequent demonstrations and an often hostile student population. The peace is brittle and the danger of new violence clear enough. London has its problems but they are not yet of that scale. If the British police were ever to form a permanent reserve it would be from necessity not from choice. It would also mean that those policies aimed at maintaining good relations with the public had failed or had been defeated.

6

Officers and Men

When Peel formed the Metropolitan Police in 1829 he made one rule which, some say, explains much of the later success of the British Police. He decreed that the new force should be made up of the public it served. As the early optimists of the French Revolution would have put it – citizen shall serve citizen. The aim was not a service like the army with its well marked divisions between officers, non-commissioned officers, and men. In the new police all the men were to be officers – or to put it more accurately all men were to be non-commissioned officers as Peel laid down that only men 'who had not the rank, habits or station of gentlemen' should be recruited. It was neither to be an elite force nor a bolt hole for the unemployable upper classes. Instead Peel wanted a professional working force where social rank took second place to ordinary understanding. The new constables certainly had to be literate but the main requirements were that they should be of good character and good physique; under thirty-five in age and over five feet seven inches in height.

In the last one and a half centuries the basic entrance requirements have changed remarkably little. At one point the height requirement went up to five feet ten inches but it has now settled back to five feet eight inches; while thirty-five remains the maximum age for a new recruit – although usually the police do not take anyone over thirty. With some reluctance the service now accept men with glasses but good physique and, of course, good character remain the pre-eminent requirements of the police recruit. Although there is an entrance test no one pretends it is unduly complicated. Nevertheless – and this is the unique characteristic of the British police – every recruit starts at the

bottom and no preference is given to the man with a good educational record. A graduate and a recruit who left his comprehensive school at sixteen without a single 'O' level to his name
start theoretically equal. It is, of course, probable that the graduate
will rise further but promotion is only guaranteed for a maximum
of twenty-five recruits a year who enter under the graduate entry
scheme – although by European standards their promotion is
hardly break-neck. They enter as constables: spend two years of
normal basic training in different police departments; move to the
Bramshill Police College for a year: return to their forces as
Sergeants: and after a further two years are automatically promoted to Inspector. This then is as far as the British police go in
providing incentives for able recruits.

The result is an equality of opportunity unparalleled in the
public service in Britain – although this has not always been the
case. Up until the last War many Chief Constables were recruited
from outside the police – often from the armed forces – and
in 1939 a count showed that only four of the English county
Chief Constables had served all their careers in the police.
But that policy has long since been abandoned as too has the
Trenchard Scheme which was the first and last attempt by
the police to provide a really ambitious management-trainee
scheme.

Lord Trenchard was himself a non-policeman who in 1933 was
appointed to command the Metropolitan Police. He had already
made his reputation as the founder of the Royal Air Force and he
swiftly set about building up his new force. As he saw it one of
the major needs was a scheme which brought on potential leaders
within the police and attracted bright young men from outside. His
critics say that this policy merely reflected his service background
and mentality but it is fair to add that Trenchard was not alone
in diagnosing a weakness in the police. A few years before in
1929 a Royal Commission had commented that the police would
only attract potential leaders 'if the system provides, and is known
to provide, prospects of rapid advancement for outstanding
young men.' In fact most of the men – 132 out of 188 – who went
under the Trenchard scheme to the Hendon police college were
serving policemen. The balance were direct recruits from outside
who spent fifteen months at Hendon and then in quick succession
served four months as constables; eight months as Sergeants; and

at least six months as Inspectors before taking command of a subdivision as a Station Inspector.*

In terms of future leaders the Trenchard Scheme was an undoubted success. In the Thirties forces were small and several Hendon men went on to become Chief Constables in their late twenties or early thirties while most Hendon graduates reached senior rank. When the Taverne Committee reported in 1967 the Trenchard Scheme could boast the Commissioner of the Metropolitan Police, the Deputy Commissioner, three Assistant Commissioners as well as twenty-one other Chief Constables. Nevertheless with the serving policeman the scheme was – and remains – violently unpopular. As the Taverne Committee remarked 'It was regarded as a deliberate attempt to create an officer class structure in the police service with the higher posts reserved for a privileged elite.'[1] To some it seemed that the British Police might for the first time be divided into officers and men – with Hendon occupying the position of Sandhurst. But the prospect soon vanished. The war intervened and after it the decision was taken to establish a national police college rather than a college run by the Metropolitan Police. The Trenchard Scheme was quietly buried.

Today the command of the police is in the hands of men who have risen from the ranks. It is true at the Police Department of the Home Office there are civil servants who have major influence but have never served with a force. Yet for all their undoubted power they do not command a single policeman. Reflecting the Home Secretary's own role they are there to advise, guide and check. In several European countries the position is fundamentally different. The highest ranks in the French police – *Directeur General, Directeurs* and *Sous Directeurs* – are filled by members of the prefectoral corps. They *are* civil servants and a senior position in the police is usually only a stage in their career: nor as some cheerfully concede do they always regard the police as one of the high spots in it. The normal top for a serving policeman would be command of an operational department like the CID or the uniformed branch. Theoretically the way to these top posts is open to even the lowliest recruit. In practice the clearly marked divisions between lower, middle and upper ranks make

---

* The scheme changed slightly over its brief life so that, for example, the training period at Hendon increased to two years; and the period as a constable lasted one year and took place before police college.

such progress unlikely – although not entirely impossible.

The rank of entry for the French recruit with no strong educational qualifications is *gardien de la paix*. Promotion is certainly open to him and at any one time there are some five thousand policemen taking correspondence courses (in their own time) to enable them to sit the promotion examinations. Nevertheless nine out of ten men who enter at this lowest rank remain non-commissioned officers for the rest of their careers perhaps progressing to *brigadier* – roughly the equivalent of a sergeant – in charge of a sub-police station with six or seven men.

Entry to the commissioned ranks is usually by examination with half the entry drawn from serving policemen and the other half from direct recruits with educational qualifications roughly equivalent to University entrance. Thus on the uniformed side there are ninety vacancies and both the serving policeman and the direct recruit take the same examination. The successful then spend eighteen months at the police school at St Cyr and pass out as *officiers de paix*. Similarly on the CID side half the *inspecteurs* are drawn from men with police experience and half from outside. It is this entry to the detective branch which is most popular with the direct entrant and demand for places exceeds supply by about ten times. It is true that the physical requirements of height and eye-sight are not as stringent as for the uniformed branch but this does not appear to be the real reason for the popularity of this form of direct entry. Physical standards still apply and even though men with glasses are recruited their eye-sight must still be reasonable. The real reason seems to be that there are a significant number of prospective recruits – many of whom have appreciably better than average educational records – who want to do CID work but not the job of the uniformed man. While it is also significant that once recruited very few of them fail to make the grade or leave because they do not like police life.

Once into the officer ranks the policeman can progress on the uniformed side up to *commandant* or even if he is particularly good up to *commandant groupement*. While on the CID side the top would be *inspecteur divisionnaire*. However, he also has the chance of winning a place in the highest ranks of all and be accepted for training as a *commissaire* – about equivalent to the British rank of Superintendent. At this level only forty per cent are drawn from serving policemen while the remainder are recruited directly from young men in their middle and late twenties with university degrees – preferably in law. Thus under the French system the graduate leapfrogs both the lower and middle ranks and, after training, goes straight to senior command.

The French rank structure then is based on the twin pillars of educational attainment and examination success. Nor is France the exception among European police forces. In spite of their democratic tradition there is still a clear division between officers and men in the Netherlands. Most Dutch policemen start as *agents* and the normal top for anyone who has joined in this way is *adjudant* – a kind of quartermaster rank between NCO and officer. Most officers on the other hand have been directly recruited and poor graduate prospects in industry produce a flood of applicants. As in France it is possible for serving policemen to become officers but promotion is difficult and in the state force less than one in ten of the officers have progressed upwards from the ranks. Not surprisingly this system is now under strong attack from the Dutch police unions and, as one union leader put it: *'the* big struggle today is to change it.'

The nearest to the British system is that of West Germany. Most German policemen start at the bottom with a two or three year training period (depending on educational qualification) at a police school. He can then win promotion to the middle ranks – the first of the officer ranks – by examination and spends a further two and a half years in training divided between police school and attachments to different sections in his force. Promotion to the upper ranks is again by examination and entails a further two years training – one year being at the national police academy at Hiltrup near Munster. To this general system there is a notable exception. As in so many things Bavaria do it their own way and that way means they will take men with degrees and put them straight into the upper ranks. Dr Manfred Schreiber the head of the now amalgamated Munich force was a lawyer; while one of the rising stars of the Bavarian police Reinhard Rupprecht was also a lawyer and spent his initial service on a world tour studying police methods in the United States and Japan.

The difference then between Britain and a country like France is fundamental. In Britain every man starts at the bottom and only a handful of graduates have even the assurance that they will reach the middle ranks. In France some policemen start at a rank which others take a life-time to achieve. Or to put it another way – the French make a god of the educational certificate: the British place their faith in practical experience. The advantage of the British system is that it has succeeded in producing a remarkably unified service. In France and Holland many policemen clearly regard the rank structure as unjust; in Britain such criticism is rare. There are, of course, policemen who believe that they should have gone further but the painstaking extended interview scheme now used for the police, as well as the civil service, means that very few potential police leaders fall through the net. Everything is now done to ensure that policemen with ability steam ahead in the British police. But do the police attract enough men of ability into the service?

Measuring ability is, of course, not easy but what is certain is that in the twenty years following the war the police almost entirely ignored one of the likeliest sources of able young recruits – the universities. As university education became more and more common in post-war Britain the competition for graduates among employers became fierce. Industry offered management trainee courses; the professions cut down periods of apprenticeship; and the armed forces emphasised that graduates were wanted and would be given responsibility quickly. Almost alone the police stood aloof. The Trenchard scheme was scrapped but nothing was put in its place. Not only was there no graduate entry scheme there was no effort made even to explain what the police offered. An undergraduate could pass through his entire university course without the prospect of a police career being put before him. Basically the police failed to adjust to the changed educational conditions of the post war world. They failed to recognize that the expansion of higher education meant that many (although by no means all) of the ablest young men would as a matter of course now go on to university.

The first uneasy stirrings came in 1962 when the Royal Commission on the Police reported that they could find 'no recent instance of a graduate joining the police.' However, it was not until 1968 that the Home Office plucked up courage to introduce their graduate entry scheme. This has undoubtedly improved the position and (as Table 1 shows) a flood of potential graduate recruits have come forward. What however is less reassuring is the evidence that even now the police find difficulty in filling all the available places although graduate unemployment appears to have improved the position for the time being.

Table 1
GRADUATE ENTRY SCHEME[2]
(Up to 25 places a year available)

	Applied	Offered Places	Joined
1972	248	26	24
1973	288	18	16
1974	210	18	12
1975	239	22	18
1976	463	20	18
1977	476	27	22
1978	319	21	20

Even among those who are recruited there are comparatively few of what the civil service examiners refer to as 'the high flyers' – the undoubted chief constables of the future. Indeed many policemen believe that the more successful graduate scheme has been the Bramshill Scholarship scheme whereby men already in the service are sent to University.* Over two hundred policemen have graduated under this scheme and (contrary to service rumour) the great majority continue to serve in the police. Certainly then the police can claim that the position has improved markedly in the fifteen years since the Royal Commission report so that by 1977 there were around nine hundred graduates in the service.

Nevertheless the problem of attracting *more* men of undoubted ability remains. The European solution of dividing the police into officers and other ranks provides no answer for the British police whose tradition is entirely different. In Britain the basic equality of promotion opportunity provides a valuable unifying force; while it is also true that the higher educational qualifications so much valued by the Europeans are acquired quicker in Britain than most other Common Market countries. A more hopeful approach would be for the police to make greater efforts in the universities explaining not only the graduate entry scheme but also the scope and job interest of a police career – together with the exceptional

* Germany also finds it hard to attract graduates and some German policemen believe that the solution would be to introduce the same kind of system there.

prospects in terms of responsibility that the police offers. What is important is that the police and the Home Office do not simply ignore this problem. It is a question easily enough swept under the carpet – for the results of neglect will not become evident until years after the current crop of ministers and chief constables have left their jobs.

However, what is equally true is that it is not enough to concentrate solely upon 'police leaders'. Here European nations share a common problem. Every police force in Europe have schemes – not only for attracting but also training police leaders. The Bramshill Police College in England runs three month courses to train inspectors and Superintendents; and a six month command course to prepare officers for the highest posts in the police service. In Germany a policeman going from the lower ranks to the middle ranks spends two and a half years in training; while a man entering the higher ranks spends a further two years. In the Netherlands men entering the higher ranks spend four years in training, three years at the national police college at Appledore and one year under professional training on the ground. While in France the national police school at St Cyr provides not only training courses for men qualifying as officers but also two year training courses for detectives – whether recruited directly or from the general police service. Yet valuable as these courses are they serve only a minority of the police.

Most recruits who join the police remain in basically the same rank for their entire careers: most British policemen remain constables and most European policemen remain in the lower ranks. Yet these are the men – the uniformed men on the ground – who actually deal with the public's problems face to face. An impression of the range of these demands is given by the Home Office's curriculum for the initial course given at police training centres. During his time at the centre the policeman must learn how to handle domestic disputes; sudden death; road accidents; fights and disturbances; and traffic control. He must also learn how to take statements; make arrests; administer cautions; and appear in court. When he leaves the training centre it is these tasks which become the staple ingredients of his job – but of course there are added problems. A policeman in London or Birmingham will have to deal with often sensitive questions of race relations; while a policeman in Paris or Amsterdam will be working in cities where part of the population can be expected to be openly hostile to him. The uniformed policeman then faces not only a difficult job but also a job where the problems he faces change relatively quickly.

It should follow then that the European forces provide both comprehensive initial training and refresher courses for their men. Sadly this is not always the case. There is still an assumption that all the uniformed man requires is experience and common sense – plus perhaps meticulous obedience to the orders of his superiors. Clearly this understates the demands on him but nevertheless training policies are based upon it – perhaps most of all in Britain. Euphemistically the British system is described as 'on-the-job' training. What this in fact amounts to is an initial training course of a mere ten weeks – fifteen weeks for policemen in London – during which the recruit is swiftly instructed on his new role. Two one hour periods are devoted to domestic disputes; three periods to arrests and cautions and four periods to fights and disturbances. Defining the objects of this initial training a Home Office working party said that the course had four main aims:

1. to provide a recruit to the police service with at least the minimum skills and knowledge which he needs to equip him for operational beat duties;
2. to build up a recruit's self-confidence and practical common sense in a way that should enable him to deal adequately and properly with members of the public;
3. to give every recruit a sound understanding of the role of the police in British society; and
4. to provide a firm base on which a programme of further on-the-job training can be developed within the constable's own force.[3]

Whether such is achieved – or even possible – in a ten week training course is clearly doubtful. Nevertheless after ten weeks the recruit is operational. It is true that his status is as a probationary constable and that he is not confirmed in the job until the end of two years. It is also true that he receives extra instruction during this probationary period – fourteen days of instruction while he is with his force and a two week course as he nears the end of his probationary period. The fact remains however that his preparation for the police takes a very poor second place to the practical training of the job itself.

Among European forces the French come nearest to the British method of training. Although men entering as officers or detectives have long initial courses the ordinary *gardien de la paix* spends no longer than five months at police school – an old barracks near the Vincennes race course in Paris where Dreyfus once awaited trial. At the school there is an emphasis on audio-visual techniques and '*au service du public*'. Following this the man enters the regular a series of films put over the message that as policemen they are police service and – after the British pattern – serves a probationary period before being confirmed.

In contrast Germany and the Netherlands put much more emphasis on initial training. A recruit in Germany with a reasonable educational background would spend the first six months of his training studying a mixture of police and general subjects at police school: he would, for example, be taught civil law and criminal procedure as well as German politics. The next year would be spent in practical training – and at the same time he would serve as a member of the stand-by police for use in emergencies. The final six months would be spent on rather more advanced police and academic training. Throughout this time the young policeman would be based on a police school – these vary from the old army barracks used by the Bremen police to the university campus setting of the police school near Nuremberg. But although based at the school the recruit no longer has to live there. Some live at home while most live at the school during the week and go home for weekends. In the Netherlands the recruit spends one year at one of the country's six training schools – although there is now some pressure among Dutch policemen to have this period extended.

Thus Britain – with the exception of one notable scheme – provides just about the shortest period of initial training of any police force in Western Europe. The scheme which is the exception is the police cadet scheme which takes young men straight from school at sixteen or seventeen and provides a general and professional training up to the age that the cadet can join a force. The scheme has been a notable success but chief constables have always set their face against recruiting more than about a third of their intake in this way. Whether this is right or wrong the reason for such a policy is revealing. It is that again the police hanker after men of worldly experience, as one put it: 'We want men who have kicked about a bit.' Doubtless there is much to be said for such an aim. What, however, this argument does not establish is the case for a skimpy initial training course.

Yet this is only part of the argument. In the same way that forces have recognized that men who gain promotion need training for their new responsibility there is a growing awareness that policemen who are not promoted need training to keep them up to date with changing conditions. In principle the case here is simple. It is a recognition that the conditions faced by policemen can change quickly and that clearly the man himself must be aware of this and how the police leaders see the response. To take an obvious example. An immigrant or foreign worker who moves into one of the cities of Europe will often come with a completely different view of the police (ranging between apprehension to hostility) than the local man. Police leaders are undoubtedly right when they say there is no substitute for a policemen's own common sense and experience but refresher training helps that common sense to be exercised. Clearly, however, the same police leaders are on strong ground when they point to the enormous practical difficulties of releasing men for such training. It is not easy for understaffed forces which are required to keep twenty-four hour cover to allow men time away. Nevertheless the difficulties should not prevent the attempt being made to steadily improve the position. For too long the man in uniform was regarded in all countries as the unskilled worker of the police. Slowly that attitude has changed – although even today policemen can be treated as simply numbers on a shift. The fact is, however, that relations between police and public depend – not so much on the men in the prestigious detective branches – but upon the thousands of men in uniform. It follows that the training made available should recognize the status and importance of the uniformed policeman's job.

7

The Policemen

If the police of Europe share one central problem it is this. In every nation the big cities provide forces with their greatest difficulties. Crime is at its most serious and both the rundown inner city areas and the new estates of tower blocks present the police with heavy case loads. Traffic is at its heaviest and if there are to be demonstrations almost invariably they will be staged in the city streets. Even the weekends provide no respite with violence on the football terraces and Friday or Saturday night drinking providing yet another task for the hard-pressed policemen. Yet it is precisely in the cities where the problems are greatest that the police over the last twenty years have experienced their greatest difficulties in recruiting local men and keeping forces up to strength.

The recession of the mid-Seventies has provided some respite but even today the story throughout Europe is basically the same. In Paris the police find it 'extremely difficult' to attract local recruits. In Copenhagen the police say 'most of our men come from the country areas. We find it much more difficult to recruit from Copenhagen itself.' In the Netherlands the greatest recruiting difficulties are experienced in Amsterdam and in The Hague. In Bavaria the police are able to recruit in the country areas on the border of Czechoslovakia but with much less success in Munich itself. In Rome the police recruit predominantly from Southern Italy. Whilst worst of all is the position in London. Here the police find it not only difficult to recruit local men but lose by resignation substantial numbers of those who do join. Indeed, over the last half century London's relative position has deteriorated. In 1919 the strength of the Metropolitan Police was 21,500 and made up one third of the British police strength: today it is 22,300 and makes up less than one fifth of the total.

Nor is there very much doubt about some of the main reasons for this position. Job opportunities are generally greater in the cities. The Munich police must compete with both the high-paying BMW motorworks and the assured regularity of the Bavarian civil service. Such opportunities are more likely to be recognized by the young man brought up in or near the cities – while by the same measure he is more likely to have formed his own view of the city force. In Paris or Amsterdam he may either share some of the common antipathy there is to the police or at very least not want to be a member of what he perceives as an unpopular force. Almost everyone today has some idea of the difficulties and dangers of police work in a city. Pictures of policemen under pressure are meat and drink to television companies and – inevitable as this may be – they hardly serve as encouraging recruiting material.

To some the solution to the city shortage is clear enough. Whether men like it or not they are drafted in from outside. This, of course, is only possible with a centrally controlled force where men can be posted from one part of the country to another. So it is that both France and Denmark follow this policy. As local policemen cannot be found to work in the capitals the newest recruits from the country areas are sent in to fill the gaps. The drawback to this policy is that although it provides men on the ground they are men who would prefer to be elsewhere. In both Paris and Copenhagen policemen impatiently count the months – or rather the years – until a vacancy occurs and they can return to their home areas. In Copenhagen a policeman can make as many as fifty applications before his transfer eventually comes through. At its best, a drafting policy is a stop gap measure. What it fails to achieve is a force made up of men with a strong local commitment to the area they police which is crucial if better police/public relations are to emerge.

In the welter of proposals advanced for improving relations between police and public it is easy to forget that probably the most important factor of all is the morale of the policemen themselves. As the 1960 Royal Commission said in their interim report: 'The police can only be expected to discharge their difficult duty of protecting the public well and conscientiously if their morale is high.'[1]

A policy of drafting men to serve the cities does not necessarily achieve that. Implicitly governments are admitting that few men given the choice would actually want to work in metropolitan areas. Yet this is not necessarily true. The cities have their advantages for serving policemen: better opportunities for promotion, higher earnings through more overtime, and certainly a wider variety of work. But these are advantages only when comparing policemen with policemen. If the city police forces are to attract and hold recruits – and that is the *only* alternative if policies of drafting are rejected – then the police service must be able to compete with outside employers.

In seeking to achieve this, it is as well to recognize some natural limitations to any policy designed to improve the conditions of serving policemen. There is no pretending that the demands of police work can be miraculously reduced. Inevitably policemen will continue to work inconvenient and irregular hours: keeping a twenty-four hour cover entails forces working in shifts. Just as inevitably this can place some strain on a policeman's family life and puts a premium on good man management. However, the police are not the only men working shifts or doing jobs which take them away from home. At the Fiat factory at Breschia in Northern Italy men work a changing shift system to keep production going round the clock five days a week and up to 1.00 pm on Saturdays. While in Bremen the river police is staffed with men who have left the German merchant navy and dropped pay – ironically to get some home life with their families.

What, however, policemen can expect is that governments do not needlessly add to the tasks that they are asked to carry out, and that wherever possible they will provide either back-up staff or get other civilian staff (like traffic wardens) to do the less skilled jobs. In Britain the picture of a policeman laboriously typing out reports with one finger may not be as common as it once was but it would be a mistake to believe that all was now well. The position in London makes the point. Over the last ten years police activity has increased and one indicator of it is the increase in arrests. In 1967 the number of arrests totalled one hundred and twenty-five thousand; by 1977 this total was over one hundred and sixty-five thousand. Such activity generates its own paper work, and an increasing need for clerical and typing staff. However, the curtailment of civil staff recruitment has meant that in London policemen have been taken off operational duties to deal with administration.

What policemen can expect also is that the financial rewards of the job recognize the difficulties of the work. Here it is interesting to compare the approach of Britain with that of three of the country's nearest neighbours – West Germany, France and the Netherlands. In Britain the 'modern approach' to pay dates from the Desborough committee of 1919 which followed the police strike.[2] Until this time police pay had been assessed in relation to the wages of an agricultural labourer or an unskilled worker. (A reasonably clear indication of how governments then regarded the policeman). Yet when Desborough reported pay compared unfavourably even with these occupations.

As the committee showed, the average pay of a married constable with two children and five years' service in a small borough force was £2.75 a week. This compared with a Newcastle tramcar driver (£3.25), a scavenger at the Mersey Docks and Harbour Board (£3.37) and a Glasgow paviour (£4.00). Breaking with the past the committee recommended that the constable should be paid above unskilled trades and the result was that between the wars the constable was paid at between fifty-five and sixty per cent above the average adult male worker in industry. The policeman became the aristocrat among workers. For not only was his pay comparatively high, he also had an assured job in a period characterized by high unemployment.

This position did not last. The post-war years brought high industrial earnings and full employment and by the time the Royal Commission was appointed in 1959 police earnings were twenty-eight per cent below average earnings in industry. The Royal Commission saved the day with an immediate pay increase and throughout the 1960s and early 1970s efforts were made to maintain the policeman's position. However, the unprecedented inflation of 1975 and 1976 – combined with the inflexibility of incomes policy – once again made police pay a critical problem. There was here a sharp comparison between the state of police morale in Britain and the position in other European countries. In Britain a dispute over an extra £6 a week provoked protest meetings and lobbies to Parliament. In countries like West Germany, Holland and France the police were markedly more content with the level of pay and some union leaders conceded privately that they were well treated.

Ironically the troubles of 1968 had a beneficial effect for these

European forces. Doubting governments were shown what could happen if the police failed and the lesson was reinforced by the appearance of urban terrorists – notably the Baader-Meinhof gang in West Germany. The result was that governments were prepared to treat the police as a special case. Britain took longer to learn that lesson and it was only when police resignations started to break all post-war records that the Government acted and set up a committee of inquiry under Lord Edmund-Davies. In July 1978 the committee presented its report. The special position of the police was recognized and immediate increases in pay proposed – which the Government agreed to implement in two stages.

The effect of the award has been to put the British police in a much stronger position. Basic pay is now more or less comparable with police pay in France and not too far behind the basic rates of the German police. Policemen in the Netherlands, however, are still some way ahead. In Britain the position following the Edmund-Davies' Report was that the basic pay for a constable ranged from £3,189 a year to £4,809. In the Netherlands the equivalent basic rate at that time ranged from £4,800 to £7,400 a year. But, as any policeman will confirm, basic pay rates are only part of the story. Special police allowances can substantially boost total earnings.

Here the British policeman has one undoubted bonus – rent allowance. This is untaxed and amounts to over £1,100 a year for a married constable in London.* Outside London the allowance is less generous and a married constable in Nottinghamshire, for example, would receive only £643 a year. Nevertheless for policemen in both cities and outside it is at least some contribution towards a mortgage payment – now that police forces generally allow men to buy their own homes. The assumption, however, that this means that policemen automatically live in the areas they police often does not hold.

Again the cities provide the chief problems. Many parts of central London are outside the price range of a serving policeman and not every policeman will want to make his home in the so-called 'problem areas'. The result is that in London the married policeman tends to commute and no longer lives in his area of service. Nor is London alone in this trend. In Paris only about a

* All figures in this chapter are at 1978 rates.

98

fifth of the policemen working in the city actually live there. Most of the remainder live between twenty and sixty kilometres from their place of work. The aim is eventually to provide low-rent police housing in Paris but in the meantime the policeman is given free travel on both rail and *metro* – a not inconsiderable benefit in itself. In addition the Paris policeman receives a rent allowance of fourteen per cent of salary; all other French policemen also receive a rent allowance depending on where they serve with the cities graded highest. In West Germany and the Netherlands there is no rent allowance but interest free loans are available for house purchase – although these loans do not cover the full price of the house.

When it comes to other allowances the European policeman is at an advantage over his British counterpart. It is true that the London policeman now receives an allowance of £650 a year but this still leaves him behind, for example, the German policeman. The German policeman receives both a special police allowance of 1,440 dms a year and a 'social allowance' which was once based on where a policeman served (in the city or village) and now is based on the number of children he has. Thus a policeman in the lower ranks receives a taxable addition to salary varying between 5,300 dms a year to over 11,000 dms a year for the man with six children. The German policeman also receives a holiday allowance; a 'thirteenth month' payment – an extra month's salary paid at Christmas – and the standard public service allowances like child allowance. In addition, he is able to benefit from an entirely free police medical service for him and his family or alternatively he will be paid three quarters of his contributions to a private health insurance scheme.

In the Netherlands there are also generous allowances. A policeman receives an irregular hours allowance amounting to fifteen per cent of his monthly salary; a holiday allowance of eight per cent of his annual salary; and like other public servants a child allowance. In France allowances amount to about one third of a policeman's total earnings. These include a special risk allowance paid to policemen (and prison staff) which amounts to twenty-two per cent of salary, and therefore the policeman on the ground, who faces the greatest risk, is paid proportionately more than senior ranks. In addition all French public servants receive a family allowance.

Yet it is not just the level of pay and allowances which is significant in any comparison. It is after all a familiar point that in any such comparison with Europe Britain tends to lag behind. The more interesting points is the *approach* of the different countries towards the police as a career. In Germany, France and the Netherlands the police go out of their way to reward experience. Again it is the Germans who lead the way.

After training the German policeman starts as a *polizeihaupt wachtmeister* and after a year becomes a *polizeimeister*. This is the basic police rank and the salary level rises by thirteen two-yearly instalments. In practice however after about five years the policeman is likely to go up to *polizeiobermeister* which is a rank which again provides thirteen staged increases. If the policeman then goes up to the next rank, *polizeihauptmeister* – the top of the lower ranks – he once more joins a rank with thirteen increases included in the structure. Thus the man who remains in the lower ranks for his police career can nevertheless look forward to regular incremental increases – quite apart from the normal annual negotiated wage settlements. While if he wins promotion to the middle or upper ranks he again enters salary bands which increase by thirteen, fourteen or fifteen stages.

The same approach is followed in both the Netherlands and France. The man from police school joins the Dutch police as *agent*. Payment in this rank goes up by twelve annual increases. However, he will almost automatically be promoted to *hoofd agent* after about five years' service and the new rank then increases by thirteen annual stages. If he is promoted to *brigadier* – the equivalent of a sergeant in Britain – he enters a rank with eleven annual increases. In France the basic *gardien* has regular two yearly incremental increases bringing him to his maximum after twenty-one years' service. However, if as likely, he goes up to *brigadier* he enters a new pay structure which brings him to a maximum after six years.

In other words the approach in these countries is to encourage the policeman to continue serving. The same policy is also followed when it comes to pension benefits. The German and French policeman can earn for himself a seventy-five per cent pension and the Dutch policeman a seventy per cent pension. While the retirement age in Germany and Holland is sixty and in France it is fifty-five. In West Germany the police have won one further benefit. Most public servants retire at sixty-five and as a result of union pressure the policeman is now paid a special gratuity of 8,000 dms to recompense him for lost earnings between the ages of sixty and sixty-five. In Holland the police have now negotiated a similar settlement with the result that a policeman is paid eighty per cent of salary and allowances between the ages of sixty and sixty-five when he finally goes onto pension. The point then is underlined that the police is a career which takes the policeman up to normal retirement age.

In Britain a markedly different policy is followed. The Edmund-Davies committee has improved the structure of the constable's pay scale but even now the position is that annual increments end after eight years and that the only further increases come after twelve years' service and fifteen years' service. As for the sergeant, he has only four incremental increases and even these only take him from £5,450 a year to £6,250. But the comparison is most marked when it comes to policy on retirement. The British pension system allows the policeman to retire after twenty-five years' service with a pension of fifty per cent of his annual salary; or after thirty years with a pension of two thirds of salary. The policeman can leave the police service once his twenty-five or thirty year spell comes to an end and the pension is payable from the age of fifty.

The British system therefore allows – or rather encourages – men to leave the police in their forties or early fifties to take up another job. As his incremental salary increases have stopped and as he has reached the maximum Treasury pension limit this would also seem to be in the best interests of the man himself. Retirement then accounts for the loss of many comparatively young men from the British police. But retirement is not the only reason men leave. Since the War the chief difficulty of the police has been the number of policemen resigning from the service before reaching the pension point. Recruitment may sometimes be difficult but resignation after recruitment has been the most intractable problem of all.

When the Commissioner of the Metropolitan Police gave evidence to the 1960 Royal Commission he told them that one third of the recruits taken into the force since the end of the War – seven thousand seven hundred out of twenty thousand two hundred – had resigned before they became entitled to a pension. In spite of the Royal Commission the problem continued throughout the

Sixties and even the unprecedented unemployment of the middle and late Seventies failed to slow down the rate. As table 2 shows men left the police for other jobs at a rate of between two thousand five hundred and three thousand six hundred a year – until in 1977 the resignations figure topped the five thousand mark for the first time. It was at this point that the Edmund-Davies inquiry was appointed.

The result of retirement policy and resignations is that today the British police are probably the youngest of the young forces of Europe. Today half the seventy four thousand constables in England and Wales are aged under thirty; twenty-three thousand are between thirty and forty; and a mere fourteen thousand are between forty and sixty. Partly this is the inevitable result of men recruited directly after the Second World War coming up for retirement at about the same time. During the war years there was no police recruitment in Britain and inevitably there was an influx once it ended. In the same way the European forces also needed exceptional numbers of recruits. Yet, having made every possible reservation the question remains whether Britain can afford to allow so many trained men to leave the police – either through resignation in their late twenties or thirties or for that matter through retirement in their forties.

The loss of experienced men is bad for the public, for the Government who have invested in their training, and, perhaps most of all, for the police service itself. The point was put by a chief constable who gave evidence to the 1960 Royal Commission:

> When I joined the police I was one amongst seventy or eighty experienced constables and I learnt from them all sorts of things which you cannot teach in schools or in text books: the experience, the knowledge of how to handle a crowd single-handed, an angry crowd turned into a good humoured crowd – all those sorts of techniques which the old policeman knew . . . now we are having new policemen trained in the service who have very little more experience than themselves.

Since then the problems faced by the police have increased and the resignation position has become worse.

What makes this position even more striking is that mass resignations appear to be an exclusively British police problem. In Paris the Ministry of the Interior say they have resignations from the

Table 2
POLICE RESIGNATIONS
(Number resigning without pension or gratuity in England and Wales)

| YEAR | Years of Service less than | | | | | | | | |
	1	2	3	4	5	10	15	25	TOTAL
1970	—	—	—	—	—	—	—	—	3,665
1971	—	—	—	—	—	—	—	—	2,610
1972	699	603	266	191	179	523	225	96	2,782
1973	770	709	362	265	225	771	288	123	3,513
1974	831	589	378	297	260	837	332	133	3,657
1975	853	520	228	169	175	481	188	87	2,701
1976	1,058	853	210	179	185	481	245	76	3,287
1977	—	2,726	—	—	939	920	447	134	5,166
1978									5,685

police during training but rarely afterwards. In Bonn a Ministry official said simply: 'we just do not have this problem'; and in both Bavaria and Bremen local police chiefs confirmed that resignations after training were unusual – and that even in training were under five per cent. In Amsterdam the police certainly face continuing difficulties recruiting the right men into the force but resignations from it do not cause a problem. So why does Britain alone suffer from the problem? One theory sometimes advanced is that it is due to bad management in the police: but few would claim that man management in the French police is better. Another theory is that it is the pressure of police work on the family: but again it is difficult to see how this differs from other European nations.

There can be no doubt that the seething discontent of the British police with their pay during the mid-1970s led to the spurt in resignations. Nevertheless it is open to question whether pay is the only reason. Certainly nothing could have been achieved without the kind of pay increase proposed by Edmund-Davies but this is not the end of the story. As the Edmund-Davies' Committee themselves said: 'It is equally important to ensure that the police service offers an attractive career. When we looked closely at recruitment it was clear that – although pay may be of great concern, especially in that if it is inadequate it is a real disincentive – other factors are of even more importance. The police officer can be expected to be looking for a career that is not only worthwhile but also offers variety and opportunities.'

This should be the next challenge: to provide for the British policeman the kind of career which keeps him in the service. Above all the aim must be to stem the resignations. Greater rewards and greater responsibility must be given to the experienced policeman and the rank structure should be reformed to give the kind of promotion opportunities there are in West Germany or Holland. As for pensions there should be no question of changing the rights of men in the service. However it is at least for consideration to examine whether it would be advantageous to encourage men to serve longer – possibly by offering a bonus to those who choose to stay after thirty years. The Edmund-Davies Committee end the introduction to their report by saying that the wider issues of the policeman's career should be kept under 'constructive joint review'. Britain should also see what lessons can be learnt from her European neighbours. The West German police have gone to enormous trouble to provide career opportunities. Is this why they are so much more successful in keeping their men? A study of European experience could provide signposts for British policy makers.

Union Power

One further point should be made about the working conditions and rewards of the police. As trade union power has increased in Europe so too has the power of the police unions. The move of Italy towards setting up a police union will mean that every country in the Common Market will have at least some representative body to put the case of the policeman – although the *gendarmerie* and *caribinieri* as basically military bodies remain exceptions. The exact organization of such representative bodies vary.

Britain has a Police Federation (divided into a federation for England and Wales and a federation for Scotland) which represents all ranks up to Chief Inspector and two small associations representing the Superintendents and the Chief Constables. But the Police Federation is not a trade union as such. The federation was formed after a brief strike by London policemen in 1918. In the subsequent Committee of Inquiry under Lord Desborough a proposal was made for 'a representative body' to discuss conditions in the different forces. The Police Act of 1919 put this proposal into effect. The federation was created but at the same time the act specified that:

> It shall not be lawful for a member of a police force to become, or after the expiration of a month from the passing of this Act to be, a member of any trade union, or of any association having for its objects, or part of its objects, to control or influence the pay, pensions, or conditions of service of any police force.

Pay was to be negotiated through a Police Council which included representatives of government, local authorities, police forces and the federation.

In the sample of Germany, Holland and France, the position is different. In Germany the biggest police union is the *Gewerkschaft der Polizei* which has a membership of one hundred and thirty-five thousand. In addition however there is the *Öffentliche Dienste Transport und Verkehr* (OTV) which is a general union – rather like the Transport and General Workers Union in Britain – which has some police members. Although numerically much weaker than GDP the OTV has one advantage; membership of the German equivalent of the Trades Union Congress which gives it an influence vastly above its actual strength. The result is that the GDP is now itself negotiating for affiliation and hopes to become the seventeenth member in the German trade union movement. GDP members are overwhelmingly in favour of such a move and the signs are that it will be just a matter of time before this is achieved.

In the Netherlands the major police union is the *Nederlandse Politiebond* which has about fifteen thousand members and is also affiliated to the Dutch trade union movement. In addition there are two police unions organized on religious lines (Protestant and Catholic); a body for senior officers, and a union for the state police. In France policemen can either join general unions, including the Communist CGT, or exclusively police unions, of which the biggest is the sixty thousand strong *Fédération Autonome des Syndicats de Police*.

Generally the unions have direct negotiating rights on pay and conditions but several unions go beyond this and seek to influence governments on general policies affecting the police. The Police Federation have had a Parliamentary Adviser in the House of Commons for a number of years (the first was James Callaghan) and policemen take part in national and local lobbies of MPs. The

German GDP have taken this approach one stage further and encourage men to join political parties and thus directly influence the policies of those parties. Such efforts to influence governments must be beyond the wildest dreams of those retired policemen who can remember the early struggles to gain even union recognition. Nevertheless such indirect means do not always satisfy the young policemen of today.

Like the public they serve, many policemen want direct means of putting pressure on governments – and such pressure includes the right to strike. In Britain the demand for such a right caused public surprise, if not shock, but in both Germany and Holland it is part of the official policy of the biggest police unions. In both nations the case put is the same. In Amsterdam a *Politiebond* official said that the strike weapon was 'the right of every worker': and in Germany a GDP official said 'The policeman is just like any other member of society and just like everybody else he should have the right to strike.' So far European governments have resisted the pressure on the grounds that a police strike would pose an undoubted threat to the state itself and the maintenance of order within it.

Nevertheless policemen in Europe have already come fairly close to outright strike action. In France there have been days of action in both 1975 and 1976. In one of these demonstrations policemen refused to handle inquiries unless life was in danger and instead handed out tracts protesting at plans to boost the *gendarmerie* at the expense of the civil police. Germany came nearest to a strike in 1970 when policemen walked out of their stations for an hour long protest; and in the same year 3,000 Dutch policemen received their director with a loud cacophony of police whistles at a meeting at the Congress Building in The Hague. While in Britain the Home Secretary was vigorously heckled by policemen at meetings in both 1976 and 1977 and at one stage a police strike seemed on the cards.

So far the worst has not happened but no government can afford to ignore what has taken place over the last twenty years. The police forces of Europe are predominantly young and the men in them have grown up in years of increasing union power. Governments then must demonstrate clearly the importance they attach to the job of the policeman and policy here must be consistent – not just responding to a particular crisis. At the same time, however, policemen should recognize their own special position. As the

Superintendents' Association said in evidence to the Edmund-Davies inquiry in 1978:

It is essential that the police service remains independent and unfettered by any political considerations or any Trade Union. This must apply right through the law-enforcement agency, from the most junior constable to the most senior judge.

It is not difficult to imagine the problems that would arise if the service had the right to strike. Presumably, when taking such action, it would be necessary to seek the support of other unions, and, conversely, there would be occasions when the service was asked to strike in sympathy – a situation that could *not* be allowed. The Service must stand apart, or we shall quickly find ourselves compromised when policing industrial disputes and police officers' sympathies are courted.

8

The Terrorist

The Munich Olympics in 1972 were to have been 'the happy games'. It was the first time that the Olympics had returned to Germany since 1936 and every German realized that comparisons would be made. In 1936 Hitler had just come to power and the Berlin games became a chilling demonstration of the new nationalism which had the country in its grip. The 1972 Games were intended to point the contrast. As one member of the local organizing committee said: 'We wanted to show the world once and for all that Germany had changed and that the old Prussian mentality had sunk without trace.' Even in the fringe events in Munich itself the aim was to reflect the international spirit of the Games. A play street was given over to folk-lore performers from around the world and among the visiting companies to the city's theatres were the Bolshoi ballet, the New York Philharmonic and the Milan opera. It was an exercise in image-making and in this exercise the police occupied a particularly sensitive position. The German authorities wanted the best of both worlds: they wanted security but with the minimum of restrictions.

Their view was that nothing would be worse than to confront the world's press and television with a police force bristling with arms, officiously overseeing athletes and spectators alike. The comment would have been instantaneous and wholly damning. It followed that the first requirement was that the police presence should not obtrude and that the policemen who were on show should, if possible, epitomize a new Germany. Nowhere was this policy taken more to heart than at the Olympic village where the athletes were housed. Security was in the hands of a two thousand strong force deliberately composed of young policemen recruited from forces throughout West Germany. Their job was to patrol and man the entrances to the village but their brief was to offer help as much as to check. Even their jaunty light blue uniforms were designed to soften the security impression. As one policeman put it: 'It was not intended to be a free village but nor was it meant to be a concentration camp.' Given this general policy it was also natural enough that physical security should not obtrude and that the perimeter fence should be seen as the surround of a village rather than a prison. It was over this low fence that eight Palestinian terrorists clambered in the early hours of Tuesday, 5 September.

From the perimeter fence they made their way straight to Block 31 which housed the Israeli Olympic team. Bursting into the first flat the terrorists shot down Moshe Weinberg, officially credited as a wrestling coach, but in fact one of the Israeli's security men. Leaving the first flat under guard the remaining terrorists next moved to the flat where the weight-lifters and wrestlers were sleeping. There they shot dead another security man and hustled the athletes below to join their colleagues. In the confusion the other members of the Israeli team in the block were able to escape and a little later a wrestling coach, Gad Isabari, was able to make a successful dash for freedom using the cover of the block's concrete supports in the basement. Nevertheless the terrorists had taken nine hostages and the happy Games had been transformed into a terrorist battleground.

For the astounded German authorities there were basically three choices of response. First they could accept the terrorists' demands and have allowed them to leave together with their hostages for Cairo. The Israeli Government, however, would only agree to this if the aircraft then flew on to Tel Aviv with the hostages. To achieve this the Germans needed an assurance from the Egyptian Government but this was not forthcoming. One policeman close to the negotiations said: 'Our information was that there was no help forthcoming from any Arab state. There was not the slightest hint of cooperation. Our view was that if we allowed the terrorists to take the hostages with them this was nothing more than a postponement of execution.' Clearly there were immense dangers in simply turning over the hostages to the mercies of their captors, and such a course would have been bitterly opposed not only by the Israeli Government but also by much world opinion. The second option open was for the police to storm Block 31 but the risk that the terrorists would simply turn their guns on the hostages was so great that it was quickly dismissed. The third course was to appear to concede to the terrorists' demands but in fact to intercept the party on its way to the waiting aircraft. The risks involved were still enormous, but it seemed the only plan which offered any hope of gaining the hostages' release.

Success depended on the police being able to pick off the terrorists before the terrorists were able to shoot down the hostages. The fewer terrorists there were the greater the chances of the plan succeeding. The trouble was that no one was quite sure how many terrorists actually there were in Block 31. The police estimate was that there were probably four, and it was not until the plan had been put into operation that it became clear there were eight. Police success also depended on the terrorists making mistakes, but this too soon appeared an optimistic assumption. The original police plan was to ambush the terrorists in the basement of Block 31 as they made their way to the helicopters which would take them to the waiting aircraft. Armed police took up their positions behind the small walls which flanked the central way through the basement. But at this point the terrorists' leader demanded to be taken over the route. The police in the basement were warned to keep down as, accompanied by Munich's head of police, Dr Manfred Schreiber, he inspected the suggested route. Had he looked over the walls he would have seen the police lying in wait but, even without doing this, he correctly came to the conclusion that the dangers were too great if the group went by foot. Instead he insisted on a bus to take both the terrorists and hostages to the helicopters and so destroyed the police's best chance of success. The first, and last, opportunity for the police came at the airbase at Fuerstenfeldbruck, just outside Munich.

The final act of the tragedy was over quickly. When the helicopters landed the hostages remained on board with two terrorist guards in each. Two other terrorists stood guard over the helicopter crew members on the tarmac; while the two remaining terrorists went to inspect the waiting (and empty) Boeing.* It was as they returned from the inspection that the police opened fire. Two of the terrorists were killed immediately, but the two others found cover in the shadow of one of the helicopters and returned

* The original plan was that ten policemen dressed as crew and maintenance men would overpower the inspecting party. However, the policemen detailed to do this admittedly dangerous job, refused.

the fire. In the lull which followed fresh appeals were made to the terrorists to surrender over the airbase loudspeakers but without effect. The stalemate lasted for almost an hour when, with the police preparing to close in, a terrorist suddenly jumped down from one of the helicopters and lobbed a grenade back into it. The police immediately opened fire and the terrorists in the second helicopter turned their sub-machine guns on the hostages. All nine hostages were now dead.

In the immediate shock following the massacre the world's press turned on the Germans and particularly the police. Why was there not better security at the village? Why did the police sharp-shooters fail to wipe out all four terrorists on the tarmac at Fuerstenfeldbruck? Why had there been no warning of the attack? The questions were endless and the criticism virtually unanimous. Yet in the welter of blame heaped on the Germans it was easy to ignore one essential fact. In spite of the death of the hostages the attack had not been a success for the terrorists. Up to this point the German authorities had stood firm. It would have been possible for them to have allowed the terrorists to take off with their hostages. Yet – quite apart from the risk involved – such action would have represented the most obvious surrender to terrorism and the clearest invitation to others to try their hand. As it was, on 6 September, five of the eight terrorists were dead and the remaining three were in prison awaiting trial. The real surrender to terrorism did not come until eight weeks later when on 29 October two Arabs hi-jacked a Lufthansa airliner and threatened to blow it up, together with the eleven passengers and seven crew, unless the three prisoners were released. In a matter of hours the German Government had capitulated with no less a figure than the Chancellor, Willy Brandt, explaining that 'the Federal Republic of Germany is not at war.' The three terrorists were flown out and the Munich tragedy was complete.

Munich was not the first terrorist challenge which Europe had witnessed. Even by 1972 Ulster had claimed many more lives than were lost at the Olympics; two years previously terrorists had forced an exchange of Arab prisoners in Europe for three hundred passengers and crew from a hi-jacked aircraft held at an airfield in Jordan; and indeed Germany itself had been battling against the increasing violence of an extreme left urban guerilla group since 1969. Yet Munich crystallized the urban terrorist problem. It showed all too clearly the vulnerability of modern society to attack. It showed how the risk of attack stretched far beyond the immediate area of political dispute. And above all it showed the difficulty of response. Munich was a watershed. Until then European governments could cling to a hope – however optimistic – that the urban terrorist was a passing phenomenon. After Munich it was a very brave or a very foolish government which refused to acknowledge that the urban terrorist was here to stay.

For the police the terrorist presents complex questions of tactics and policy which go to the heart of their relationship with the public. The demand of the public is that the police should protect those targets that they consider important; and that the police should take swift and certain action against terrorists when they reveal themselves. The most obvious complication is that the number of targets for the terrorist is virtually limitless. The terrorist may just as easily strike at an international games, a parliament building, an airport or an embassy – to say nothing of art galleries, museums and television studios. An attack on any of these will attract attention to his cause and can usually provide a lever on government in the form of hostages, victims or objects of ransom. Governments have now recognized the threat and this in its turn has led to new demands on police manpower. In June 1974 Sir Robert Mark, the Commissioner of the Metropolitan Police, reported an increase in requests for police protection from foreign governments with embassies in London. But as he also commented, this new demand placed not only a demand on manpower but a 'severe strain on the morale of the officers involved.'[1] While in Paris also it is a major complaint of the police trade unions that too often policemen are used as security guards. The fact is that no policeman likes being employed merely as a guard, particularly in a situation where no police force can expect to guard everything which is open to attack. Thus if the police place too much emphasis on providing static guards they run the risk of provoking resignations from within the service without satisfying the public demand for protection. The next complication is that in taking that certain action necessary to destroy operational terrorists the police must pursue means which some of the public will consider conflict with their other roles. The same force must contain community policemen and men trained to kill. In Britain this poses particular problems.

Britain's ability to maintain a predominantly unarmed police is a cause of both admiration and wonderment in Europe. Among European forces fire-arms are the rule, and any attempt by Government to send men on duty without them would be fiercely resisted by the police themselves. In Germany after the war the police were rearmed before the army, and as one German policeman put it: 'We will disarm when we see signs of the criminals giving up their guns.' Nor is it just policemen who are armed. In several European countries the law also allows the staff of the private security companies to carry guns. In Belgium most security guards employed on cash in transit are armed. While in France, guards are armed and vans so heavily armoured that, according to one security man in Paris, an attempt at interception 'would not be so much an attack as a duel.' In most European countries then it is accepted that the threat of criminal attack justifies the police in carrying arms. In Britain the tradition of the unarmed police is valued by public and policemen alike.

This policy (like so much else) dates from the formation of the police itself and the decision that the policeman should be as little different as possible from the ordinary member of the public. Over the years it has meant that the public generally have felt a sense of responsibility for the police whom it is acknowledged have often to face danger without protection; and there is genuine outrage when a policeman is killed on duty. It has also led to the belief that fewer criminals than otherwise carry guns. This theory has been rather dented by the increase in offences involving fire-arms – for example the number of armed robberies in England and Wales increased from two hundred and sixty-five in 1967 to over twelve hundred in 1977. Yet even so, the use of fire-arms is less common in crime in Britain than in either Germany or France – and dramatically less than in Italy.

The British policy, however, has always been subject to some exceptions and the advent of the terrorist has produced the most serious challenge so far to the principle itself. Public attention was first turned seriously to this question at the end of 1972 after a Kensington bank robbery. During the robbery the bank's alarm went off, and a policeman who was on his way to armed duty outside one of the foreign embassies in Kensington rushed into the bank. When he saw that the robbers were armed he called on them to surrender, and opened fire when a shotgun was fired at him.

113

Although wounded himself he fired again and this time shot and killed one of the gang whose body was found shortly afterwards in a nearby carpark. It was, of course, complete chance that an armed policeman should have been passing, but it served to establish to the public that the terrorist threat meant that some British policemen were now armed as a matter of course. No longer was it simply a question of policemen drawing arms for an emergency. Some policemen (albeit a small minority) now carried guns for every day duty. The point was underlined only two months later when two Pakistani youths who made an attack on the Indian High Commission in London armed with replica guns were both killed by armed policemen whose responsibility was again to guard vulnerable diplomatic buildings.

The terrorist threat then has forced a change – at least of emphasis – in British policy. Although most policemen remain unarmed, some specialist groups can now carry guns. The police who guard embassies and other likely targets can be armed and the same is sometimes (although by no means always) true of members of the Special Patrol Group in London. This group was formed in 1965 as a mobile reserve force for the Metropolitan Police able to help with any police emergency from a local crop of burglaries to handling the crowd at a football match. In its early days the group helped the CID to break up the Kray and Richardson gangs, and they have also provided extra manpower for working with the serious crime squad. Their counter-terrorist role started in 1970 when they provided special units for Heathrow Airport and in 1972 – after an attempt to assassinate the Jordanian Ambassador – they helped provide a watch on embassies. Most of the men now receive arms training and in an emergency the group can provide a well-trained force including its own sharp-shooters – who are, in the main, arms instructors. Yet even today the British police role is restricted. As a general rule the police would only deal with the more minor terrorist strikes, but if there was evidence that the terrorists were able to use substantial fire power then the operation would become one for the army acting under civil control. Thus at Heathrow the army is periodically called in following intelligence reports that terrorists could mount a major operation. So where does the police end and the army begin?

Normally the army in Britain has no part in handling internal crises and maintaining order but, as in other European countries, this rule can be broken. The army can be called in to help with disaster relief (Military Assistance to the Civil Community); to keep essential services going during a strike (Military Assistance to the Civil Authorities); and when public order would otherwise break down (Military Assistance to the Civil Power). It was in this last role that the army were sent to Ulster in August, 1969, when communal and simultaneous violence in Londonderry and Belfast finally established that the three thousand strong Royal Ulster Constabulary (RUC) was unable to cope with a situation which was fast approaching insurrection.

The RUC occupied a difficult, if not impossible, position in Northern Ireland. They were required to carry out both a civil police and military role with a strength which was sufficient for neither. When the two communities started on their six month marching season of religious and political processions thousands of Ulstermen would flock onto the streets. In Belfast alone the procession of 12 July, with which the Protestant Orangemen celebrated the Battle of the Boyne in 1690 and the defeat of the Catholic James II, could attract a crowd of ten thousand marchers and spectators. To control such a mass the police in Belfast had a strength of one thousand two hundred. While at Londonderry, close to the border with the Irish Republic, the RUC strength was one hundred and twenty-three.

In 1969 the RUC was the only police force in the United Kingdom which was armed and the only force equipped with armoured carriers and water cannons. It is easy enough to criticize this policy but the long list of murdered policemen on the roll of honour at the RUC headquarters in Belfast makes it easily understood.

It is possible that had an attempt been made to introduce an unarmed police in Northern Ireland in the period of comparative calm in the early and mid-Sixties, this could have gone some way to encouraging acceptance by the Catholic community of what was a predominantly Protestant force. Certainly some of the RUC – although by no means all – would have welcomed such an attempt, but the opportunity was lost. When Sir Arthur Young took over command of the RUC in October 1969 and attempted to introduce an unarmed police it was too late.

The break point for the RUC came in Belfast on the night of Thursday, 14 August. An ugly riot had developed in Divis Street

in West Belfast which roughly marked a boundary between Protestant and Catholic homes. Provocation by a large group of
Catholic youths carrying a tricolour and singing the Irish Republic's national anthem had led to a Protestant counter-attack
which was pushing into the Catholic territory across Divis Street.
Suddenly shots rang out and a protestant, Herbert Roy, was
mortally injured and three policemen hurt. At this point the
police decided to deploy three of their Shorland armoured cars
which were armed with Browning machine guns. The fire had
appeared to come from the block of flats overlooking Divis Street,
and this now became the police target. At least one of the
Shorland's opened fire and several bursts of machine gun fire
sprayed the flats – accidentally killing a nine year old boy, Patrick
Rooney. While immediately following the Shorland firing a police
marksman shot dead Hugh McCabe, a British soldier home on
leave, who was on the roof of the flats.

In the subsequent tribunal of inquiry, under Mr Justice Scarman,
both the deaths caused by the police were exhaustively investigated.[2] In the case of McCabe the tribunal found that the police
action was justified. McCabe had been throwing down missiles at
the police from the roof of the flats and there is no doubt also that
some shots were also fired from the roof. The tribunal found that
the police target was a legitimate one, and that after McCabe's
death there was no further firing from the roof of the flats. On the
death of the nine year old boy, however, the tribunal were highly
critical. In the case of McCabe the shooting consisted of single
shots carefully and skilfully aimed; in the case of Patrick Rooney
the police had fired bursts indiscriminately into the central area
of a block of flats. It was not that the men in the Shorlands had
deliberately set out to kill; it was rather that they had been confronted with a situation which had become too big for them to
handle. Quite clearly Ulster had become a job for the army.

In Northern Ireland today policing continues – thanks to the
exceptional courage of the men and women of the RUC. Yet
although the force carry weapons for their own protection, armed
operations against terrorists remain firmly in the hands of the
army. Given the level of violence in Ulster – which places it quite
apart from the rest of the United Kingdom – there are few who
would seriously dispute that policy. The division between police
and army becomes more difficult when governments are faced

by more limited and periodic threats. In every country in the Common Market the basic every-day work of guarding likely terrorist targets and, for that matter, collecting intelligence, is in the hands of the police. What, however, happens when there is an exceptional threat of terrorist force? Is that a job for the police or the army?

The Munich Olympics was a good test case. As Dr Richard Clutterbuck has pointed out the attempt to intercept the Palestinian terrorists at the Fuerstenfeldbruck airbase called for 'a tactical attack by a trained team of soldiers using fire and movement; that is one group firing to pin the guerrillas down while an assault group on foot or in armoured vehicles, closes in from a flank to kill or capture the guerillas.'[3] Nevertheless, the Munich operation was carried out by the police, and one view is that it was the lack of military skill of their marksmen which ruined the whole operation. The marksman is a specialist, and as one senior Munich policeman close to the operation said: 'You not only need men with special weapons, you also need men under continual training. To produce real sharp-shooters you have to take men out of normal police work.' The police marksmen used in 1972 simply had not been trained to that standard. Equally, the refusal of the police to man the waiting Boeing could well have proved disastrous and was clearly intolerable in an anti-terrorist action.

The Germans have now sought to overcome this problem by, in effect, training policemen as soldiers. At the federal level a special anti-terrorist squad has been formed out of members of the border guard. Members of the squad are trained not only as marksmen but also to handle other terrorists' actions like the hijacking. Each state can call in the squad in an emergency – although in addition every state has a police commando squad of its own. But, of course, the position in Germany is very different to that in Britain. The border-guard is a para-military force, and the German police are armed as a matter of routine. Britain has no third force between the police and the army, and instead follows a policy whereby the police deal with the limited terrorist threat and the army with situations where sophisticated weapons and specialized training are necessary.

In practice this means that the police deal with situations like the Balcombe Street and Spaghetti House sieges in London in 1976 where terrorists had taken hostages, but where there was no possibility of escape. Operations remain under the police and although there is clearly liaison between the Government and the police, it is the Commissioner of Police who remains in charge. But, as Sir Robert Mark has pointed out, the police 'are equipped only to deal with armed criminals and political terrorists *not* posing any extraordinary problem.'[4] In the case of 'extraordinary' threat the army are called in and the police play a supporting role. In Britain it would have been the army and not the police who would have gone into action at Fuerstenfeldbruck in 1972 and – as, unlike the police, the Government directly control the army – the line of command would go directly to the Minister of Defence.

Thus even in its response to terrorism Britain has taken a cautious stance. The police have a limited armed role but not so pronounced as to interfere with their reputation as a civil force serving the community. The army is called in only in exceptional cases, thus allaying any public concern that it is interfering in the internal affairs of the state. It is an arrangement which depends on complete co-operation between police, army, Home Office and Ministry of Defence and if that co-operation was ever to be missing then the results could be disastrous.

Yet the British system recognizes an important truth. Britain bases its counter-terrorist strategy on the minimum force necessary to meet the threat. It can be argued that this is an approach which does not result necessarily in the most certain response and that in the conditions of today the public would accept a stronger role for either the police or the army. But public goodwill – even in dealing with terrorism – should not be taken for granted. The aim of the terrorist is to influence minds, and often it will suit his book to demonstrate 'repressive' authority. Like the demonstrators of the late Sixties they want to provoke governments into what they can portray as 'over-reaction'. As Robert Moss has pointed out 'one of the heaviest burdens for a democratic society confronted with terrorism is that government action will be judged by moral and legal standards that the terrorists do not apply to themselves.'[5] In 1972 the major reason why there was so little security at the Munich Games was that the authorities feared the public reaction to the checks which would have been necessary. Today there is no question that the public's view has changed dramatically – but governments should always remember that in another few years public opinion could have easily changed again.

Terrorism then has become an essential part of modern police work. Every nation in Europe now takes some form of protective measures. France has special police anti-terrorist squads within the police and the *gendarmerie*; and in Italy also policemen are trained to handle terrorist operations. Nor are the precautions confined to the big nations of Europe. In the Netherlands there are special task forces with men trained both in sharp-shooting and hand-to-hand combat; while the police in Belgium also train their men in the same way. The threat is recognized, and in February 1975 Interpol (The International Criminal Police Organization) held its first international symposium in Paris on 'cases involving hostages'. Information was exchanged on the technical methods of combating the terrorist but, ironically, it was the French delegate who pointed out that technical improvements were not enough. He suggested that all nations should make their attitude on terrorism clear to the terrorists because at present there were 'hard line governments and other governments more likely to satisfy the criminals' demands.' The full irony of the French delegate's remarks only became clear two years later.

In January 1977 Abu Dauod was detained in Paris as the suspected organizer of the terrorist attack at the Munich Olympics. The arrest was carried out by the French counter-espionage service DST (who had themselves lost two men, murdered by the pro-Palestine guerrilla 'Carlos') on information supplied by the West German police and on a warrant issued by a Munich judge. Four days later Abu Dauod was free and on an aircraft to Algiers. According to the French Government the reason for the release was the warrant from Munich had not been accompanied by extradition papers sent through the diplomatic channels. It was an explanation, however, which few outside the Arab world accepted. The Germans protested that they were working on the extradition procedure and, unofficially, attacked the French for the break-neck speed with which Abu Dauod had been set free; while the Israeli Government (themselves working on an extradition request) condemned the decision as a surrender to political pressure and the threats of terrorist organizations.

The Abu Dauod affair shows that Europe still has some way to go in combating terrorism. There is little point in forming anti-terrorist squads to protect the public, if governments have not the political will to stand firm. The only policy for Europe which makes sense is a common policy of 'no deals' – for unless such a policy is followed, it is foolish of governments to believe that the police, or indeed the army, can save them. That such a policy can work was shown in October 1977 when the West German Government refused to release thirteen terrorist prisoners in exchange for over eighty passengers on a Lufthansa Boeing. Using the special force created in the direct aftermath of the 1972 Olympics the aircraft was stormed and the passengers released. It would be foolish to believe that every anti-terrorist operation will be such a clear and spectacular success. Nevertheless the strategy is the only strategy which holds out any hope for the defeat of terrorism. Five years after Munich West Germany showed an example to the rest of Europe.

9

Crime and the Law

There is little doubt about which country in West Europe faces the worst crime problem. Since 1950 the number of crimes in Italy has trebled but what sets this increase apart from other nations where over the same period crime has also trebled is the kind of crime now being encountered. It is the most serious crimes which have increased (and are increasing) fastest and there is no mistaking the gravity of Italian serious crime. In 1973 there were 1,735 armed robberies with banks, post offices and supermarkets as the usual targets: by 1976 the total had increased to 4,300. Another group of crimes showing an alarming increase were attacks classified by the police as 'con movente politico' (with political motives). These range from attacks on judges or police to extortion when in Mafia style businessmen are threatened that unless they 'contribute' their businesses will be destroyed. In 1974 this group of crimes totalled 482; by 1976 it had increased to 1,198 cases – 235 cases involving the use of bombs. While on top of this there is an average of over fifty kidnappings a year which has forced some of the wealthy (and thus the likeliest targets) to take out legally questionable insurance policies in case of ransom demands. Thus each week in Italy there are on average eighty armed robberies, twenty-four cases of extortion, and one kidnapping. Nor is this even an end to it. For in 1976 three hundred and fifty of those arrested for major crime succeeded in escaping from prison.

Not surprisingly then many observers see Italy as trembling on the abyss. The nearest comparison to the Italian situation, it is pointed out, is Ulster and there the army has been called in to preserve the province from chaos. In Italy terrorists, extremists from left and right, and armed robbers (all rightly recorded in the statistics as criminals) have combined to present a profound challenge to the police and the other law enforcement agencies. In 1974 the Italian delegate to a European conference of Interpol reported that the police had been almost 'overwhelmed' by the crime wave: since then the position has become measurably worse. Italy then stands on the extreme – but there are elements of the Italian situation to be found in every other West European country.

As we have seen terrorism is unquestionably a common problem and over the last thirty years Europe has shown a similar upwards trend in most other crimes – confounding the hope of those who believed that when peace and prosperity returned crime would automatically turn down. Sir Leon Radzinowicz put the point:

In the early fifties it appeared that the hope would be fulfilled: with better education, the welfare state, full employment, it seemed that criminality would be starved at the roots. Nothing of the kind: as the golden curve of affluence gathered momentum the black curve of crime did the same.[1]

However measured and over whatever period the figures tell the same story. In 1950 the number of crimes in England and Wales per one hundred thousand of population was one thousand and forty-eight; and in Scotland the figure was one thousand four hundred and forty-four. By 1975 both the English and the Scottish figures (which are not identically defined) had increased to over four thousand offences per one hundred thousand. (As Table 3 shows, for the first time the English crime rate is now higher than the Scottish). In West Germany the crime rate in 1963 was two thousand nine hundred per one hundred thousand: the latest figures show it as over four thousand seven hundred. While in the Netherlands where at the end of the 1960s the crime rate was still only one thousand eight hundred and forty crimes per one hundred thousand the rate is now approaching three thousand five hundred. Even in the last five years the increases have been massive – in West Germany the crime total has increased by a fifth; in England and Wales by almost forty per cent; and in the Netherlands by an incredible seventy per cent. While beneath the visible mass of recorded crime is a dark area of hidden crime ranging from undetected shop-lifting and staff-theft to murders recorded as accidents or suicides.

The figures then indicate the broad trend of crime in different European nations. But to go one stage further and make exact

Table 3
CRIME RATE IN ENGLAND AND WALES

	1930	1940	1950	1960	1970	1975
Indictable crimes	147,031	305,114	461,435	743,713	1,555,995	2,105,631
Population ('000s)	39,801	41,862	44,020	45,775	48,988	49,219
Offences per 100,000 of population	369	729	1,048	1,625	3,176	4,278

CRIME RATE IN SCOTLAND

	1930	1940	1950	1960	1970	1975
Crimes made known	36,723	62,266	74,640	102,617	167,223	212,540
Population ('000s)	4,828	5,065	5,168	5,177	5,214	5,206
Offences per 100,000 of population	761	1,229	1,444	1,982	3,207	4,083

international comparisons is notoriously difficult. To compare the number of crimes with the total of population provides a reasonably accurate national index but simply to compare the crime rate in one country with another can be dangerously misleading. Such a comparison would show, for example, that Italy's crime rate of one thousand five hundred offences per one hundred thousand of population in 1950 had increased to three thousand six hundred in 1975. Thus it would be possible to reach a finding that crime had increased faster in Britain than in Italy; that the crime problem itself in Britain was worse; and that the public in West Germany was most at risk from criminal attack. But the validity of such comparisons would depend upon what offences found their way into the national statistics and the efficiency of police forces in recording crime – West Germany records crime more exactly than most.

Currently there is no ideal method of resolving these difficulties. But what it is possible to do is to examine the trends by isolating a number of crimes which are likely to be defined in the same way in each European country and to be least affected by different police recording practices. A guide here is provided by the annual returns sent to Interpol in Paris. Each country is asked to break down its figure into six groups – murder, sex offences, larceny, fraud, counterfeit currency and drug offences. There is a further subdivision of larceny between major larceny (armed robbery, burglary, housebreaking) and minor larceny. What then do these figures show about broad trends of European crime?

A comparison of the Interpol returns from West Germany, the Netherlands, France and England and Wales reveals that the only group of offences which has shown any tendency to reduce have been the sex offences. Fraud offences (which are very substantial in number) are tending to rise while drug offences have shown a steep rise during the Seventies. The murder rate (as defined by Interpol to include infanticide) has increased although less fast than some other crimes of violence and the number of murders still remains small in total. But without doubt the most significant increase in each nation has been in serious larceny. For example in the Netherlands serious larcenies increased from fifty thousand a year in 1970 to one hundred and fifteen thousand a year in 1975. The significance of this trend is that it is the crimes which the public themselves perceive as most important and which are most likely to have an impact on their own lives which are now increasing fastest.

Reviewing the British position in the mid-Seventies Sir Robert Mark, the then Metropolitan Police Commissioner, said:

The real problem emerging from the statistical fog is the significant increase in selective crimes of violence: of planned robbery and burglary directed at particular targets in which firearms or other weapons are carried. The number of the latter is still not large in comparison with, for example, the United States but the trend is worrying.[2]

In Britain the trend has continued. There was a thirteen per cent increase in robbery in England and Wales between 1976 and 1977 and in some areas the increase was between thirty per cent and forty per cent. In the same period burglary went up by eighteen per cent leading the Chief Inspector of Constabulary to comment that 'unless homes are turned into fortresses the determined burglar will have his successes'. In other Common Market countries the trend has been the same. In October 1973 the French were forced to set up a central office 'pour la repression du banditisme' after a rapid increase in armed robberies but in spite of this the figures have continued upwards. While in the Netherlands – which did not experience its first bank robbery until 1965 – there are now three or four robberies a week aimed at banks, post offices or supermarkets. Nor are the criminals always Dutch. One policeman in the Hague said: 'There are now no national frontiers as far as crime is concerned. Traditionally Holland has been a peaceful country without too much emphasis on the police. But today professional criminals are always looking for the weakest link in the chain of continental countries'.

Yet although it is true that there are now an increasing number of internationally organized crimes – an Interpol working party met in May 1975 to consider the question of robberies and burglaries prepared outside the target country while drug trafficking has always been international – most crime is homespun. The criminal who causes most concern to the police is not so much the international thief but the domestic professional criminal. Most of all this is the case in Britain where the international criminal (because of language and the relative difficulty of crossing the national frontier) has little impact. The professional criminal, on the other hand, has become a prime police target. One London policeman sought to define him:

He's been through all the graduate ceremonies possible and one evaluates him on his ranking by other top class villains. He is flexible. He will probably be in long firm fraud . . . and possibly mucking about with currency. He may be organising intelligence for other criminals like how he can place his hands on a bent bank clerk or a bent security man. That kind of job is very organised – and it is organised by top class villains. They have the money and the time and the patience to do it. They may even move into a legitimate business as a cover.

A commander at Scotland Yard added to the picture:

Some of these people are living pretty affluently. They haven't got a £10,000 house in Lewisham. They have got a £40,000 home in Surrey. Some of them have a semi legitimate business, a green grocers, a haulage contractor. Basically it would be legal but it would be the front – the way to show his neighbours that he is earning an honest living and paying his taxes.

In 1974 a case at the Old Bailey went a long way to establishing the accuracy of the police sketch. The trial centred on two major bank raids in Ilford and Wembley in which £375,000 was stolen. Before the trial one of the robbers turned Queen's Evidence and largely as a result of this seven men were sentenced to a total of 113 years imprisonment. At the Old Bailey the picture which emerged was of a tightly contained criminal community whose members had a well-developed belief in their own immunity to arrest and conviction. Raids were carefully planned and then executed without any compunction for those who might be standing in the way. What also emerged was that several of the robbers were not only living dual lives but had pretensions to respectability. One robber formed a small property company and was the captain of his local golf club; another had set himself up as a farmer in Cornwall and was known for his generosity to local charities.[3] It is, of course, true that men like these are not the *average* criminal. The average criminal in terms of numbers is male, under twenty-one and likely to be caught and convicted. In Britain two out of three known burglars are under the age of twenty-one and three out of five robbers: while every second offender who is convicted in court is a recidivist. But eventually after a number of convictions the average criminal gives up. The professional criminal may also have previous convictions but he persists in the belief that on average he will succeed – and too often he does.

The theory of police work is not that efficient detective work can stop crime – that would be an absurdly unrealistic goal – but that in company with other policies they can make an effective contribution to preventing some crime. The deterrence of detection is an essential part of the police creed. Again it is Radzinowicz who has set out the theory clearest:

> For every kind of offence there is one group of people to whom it is almost unthinkable; another to whom it is almost irresistible; and a third who might indulge in it if the temptation got too great or the risk too small. I think economists talk about marginal producers – those who will come in when the profits are high and the risks are low and who will be the first to drop out if profits fall or risks rise. Perhaps we also have marginal offenders and perhaps it is these who are the main target of general deterrence. At the same time we cannot afford to neglect the big boys of crime: it is they who most expand their operations when they see the profit vastly outweigh the risk . . . It is they who set the pace.

Yet whatever the theory the position in Europe today is that there is not one major country which claims to get to the bottom of more than half its recorded crime. West Germany claims most with a clear up rate approaching five crimes out of ten. In France, and Britain, six crimes out of ten go undetected; in Italy and the Netherlands the figure is seven crimes out of ten; and in Denmark only one crime in four is now cleared up.

However, as all police forces are quick to point out, the position is not qualitatively as bad as the crude averages suggest. With some crimes the average clear-up rate is much higher. In London, for example, where the general clear-up rate is below one in four the detection rate for offences against the person (murder, attempted murder, manslaughter, rape) is eight or nine out of ten. The same is true in other European forces. The German police solve over ninety per cent of all murders, as do the police in France and the Netherlands. The Italian police do not do as well with murder – although they clear up two thirds of such cases – but they have a noticeably high rate of success with sex offences where the detection rate is almost ninety per cent. The figures then establish a further point about police work: as no police can expect to solve all crime, forces work to a scale of priorities. At the top are crimes like murder; at the bottom are crimes like stealing from a car. Few would dispute the inevitability of such a development given the evidence that nations like Britain, France, Germany and Italy are all facing crime totals exceeding two million offences a year. Nevertheless what the police have been unable to do is to make the same impact on all the crimes which the public would take seriously. In London the detection rate for house burglary is little more than one in ten and the position is no better in Paris, Munich or Amsterdam. While the robber still continues to enjoy a high degree of impunity in every nation – no major nation claims a clear-up rate of more than four out of ten. Yet robbery has become the distinctive offence of the European professional criminal.

Faced with this challenge the police have responded in the only way open to them – they have formed specialist squads. In London a robbery squad was formed by the Metropolitan Police in the Autumn of 1972; while the French formed their unit in Paris a year later. In both cases the aim was to collect intelligence upon the criminals who were believed to be active robbers and both operated on the principle that, as one London policeman put it, 'if you put enough men with experience on the job then you are liable to get results.' The trouble is, that this is not an infinitely extendable theory. If a police force forms a squad to deal with robbery then unless men can be found from elsewhere, other work will suffer. Yet forces are often overstretched in those other areas. At the time that London formed its robbery squad research showed that the local detective used in the division (say in Chelsea or Fulham) had three hours to solve a burglary before he was asked to investigate another burglary. As one policeman complained 'unless the burglar is caught in the act or very soon after he will probably get away with it.' The choice then for European governments is fairly clear. They can give forces the money to increase their strength or they can accept that the public will be required increasingly to look after itself when it comes to minor and not so minor crime. As far as detective work is concerned the present picture is of nations getting dangerously near to minimum level services – concentrating upon the undoubtedly serious and the emergency (even then not always successfully) while progressively being forced to ignore the minor or at most give it perfunctory attention. While as if this was not enough policemen in several countries make one further complaint – the difficulty of obtaining convictions of the guilty in the courts.

This, of course, is an area which can offer no certainty. As one London lawyer said: 'how can policemen know which men are guilty? That must be the decision of the court.' Clearly the lawyer is substantially correct: the police state arrives when policemen decide guilt or innocence. The point, however, which is being put is considerably more moderate. The case put by some policemen today is that as well as protecting the rights of the innocent, governments must also concern themselves with protecting the public. The public's rights, they argue, are not protected if the legal system makes it possible for the guilty to escape. In other words there is a balance to be struck – and the balance is not achieved by simple repetition of the attractive catch-phrase that 'it is better for nine guilty men to escape than that one innocent man should be convicted.' For as Chadwick pointed out 150 years ago there is a powerful counter-argument: 'It should be borne in mind that the escape of one delinquent must do more mischief than the conviction of perhaps half a dozen guilty men can effect good in the way of example'. Chadwick was talking of the police role in

128

detection of criminals but it must follow that there is little point in
police forces working to this aim if they cannot obtain convictions.
The point then to be examined is whether the balance has shifted
too far in favour of the accused?

In West Germany many policemen believe it has. As is the case
in nearly all European countries German criminal law is based on
the inquisitorial principle. The court in effect investigates the case
during the trial and (in theory) the object becomes the pursuit of
truth in which both public prosecutor and defence counsel co-
operate. The system, as one German jurist put it, is

> . . . designed to prevent the defendant's fate from depending
> upon the ability, ready wit, dialectical skill and degree of energy
> and ruthlessness which prosecutor and defence counsel as op-
> posing parties are able to muster against the witnesses of the
> other side. It prevents the degeneration of the trial into a kind
> of duel where guilt or innocence of the defendant is at stake.[4]

Such assumptions, however, depend upon their total acceptance
by prosecutor and defender. According to defence counsel public
prosecutors (who are in a distinct career and have responsibility
for over-seeing criminal proceedings from the preliminary enquiry
to the final trial) all too rarely follow this course. The law places
on the prosecutor a duty 'to discover, and to submit, all the points
incriminating and exonerating the accused.' According to one well
paid defence lawyer whose outer office was hung with photographs of some of his most newsworthy cases, once the public
prosecutor has decided to take proceedings he seeks a conviction –
'it becomes *his* case.'

The police, however, are more concerned by the activities of
defence counsel and, although this is scarcely surprising, their concern is supported by objective evidence. Following the War the
new rules set down for criminal investigation and procedure put
understandable emphasis on the freedom of the individual and the
protection of his rights. Twenty-five years later when some of the
Baader-Meinhof terrorist gang went on trial in Stammheim prison
in Stuttgart some of the same rules were used by defence lawyers to
prolong the trial for almost two years from May 1975 until April
1977. During it the five judges were at times forced to leave their
own court – the exclusion of a defence lawyer for misconduct
cannot be settled there and then but must be referred to another

court – and although convictions were at last obtained very few Germans can be happy about the process.

Just before his assassination in 1977 Herr Siegfried Buback, the Federal Attorney General gave an interview to *The Times* correspondent in Bonn. During it Herr Buback referred him to an article in the German Judges' Journal which drew comparisons with a number of American cases when 'defendants made common cause with their clients'. According to some German policemen (and many others besides) this on occasion is what has happened in West Germany. In a few cases lawyers have actually joined terrorist groups (one lawyer Horst Mahler was a founder of the Red Army Faction) or co-operated with them in acting as links between detained terrorists and accomplices outside. But the more basic challenge comes from the more numerous lawyers whose conduct in the words of Dan van der Vat: '. . . has never gone beyond the bounds of propriety but who exploit all the weaknesses of the law for their clients with unprecedented zeal. They use their wiles and legal and procedural loopholes in such a way that a trial can rapidly degenerate into an embarrassing shambles.'[5]

Another country facing difficulties in obtaining convictions of the guilty is Italy. The Italian position is first complicated by the delays in the legal system. Over the last four years, the courts (who lack magistrates and court staff) have simply not been able to keep pace with the increase in crime. The result is that in the higher courts (the *corti di assise*) the average time between arrest and the end of the trial is one year: while an appeal will take on average 470 days to be heard. In the second division courts (which have a sentencing power of up to six years imprisonment) it takes on average six hundred days between the arrest and the result. The effect of these delays is felt both by the accused and the police. For the accused it can mean long periods spent in custody waiting for trial; for the police it means that their witnesses are open to the obvious defence challenge that after such long periods recollection can only be hazy. Intimidation of court and witnesses presents a further obstacle to Italian justice and means that trials of terrorists in particular take place only under the most severe difficulties. While Italian policemen also complain that legal reforms over the last ten years have left them unduly hampered. The old criminal procedure meant that policemen were able to question every suspect and every witness to a crime but the process was secret and led to complaints that the police were abusing their power. As a result of this criticism the rules were changed so that now a policeman cannot question a suspect who has been arrested on the facts of the case but must bring the arrested man before a magistrate. The police criticism of this new procedure is twofold. First they claim that the magistrate is less skilful in obtaining statements, and second that the requirement of the magistrate's intervention delays interrogation and means that the suspect has recovered his self-composure. In other words the complaint is again that the balance has been tipped too far in the favour of the accused.

In judging whether the same is also true of Britain it is important to dispose of two initial questions – the fundamental difference between the inquisitorial and accusatorial systems of law; and the substantial difference in procedure within Britain itself. The general system followed in the Common Market is the inquisitorial and the clearest example of it at work is the French criminal procedure. The procedure is that all the facts concerning both the offence and the person alleged to have committed it should be placed before the court. This aim is achieved by making detailed pre-trial enquiries; by examining the personality of the accused; and by placing the onus of eliciting the evidence at the trial on the judge rather than on the parties to the case. In the most serious cases the pre-trial enquiries are placed in the hands of an independent *magistrat* known as the *juge d'instruction*. He, rather than the senior policeman assigned to the case, actually directs the investigation and his responsibility is to gather facts which are both against the accused and in his favour. The pre-trial investigation does not seek to pre-judge the case but rather to compile a *dossier* which will go before the court if the *juge d'instruction* decides to press charges. If charges are made then the *dossier* is handed to the president of the court and although not restricted to it, he will follow substantially the results of the inquiry. The duty of eliciting the evidence is given to the judge – rather than the opposing counsel – and as all relevant evidence is admissible this will include evidence of previous convictions. At the end of the trial the judge retires with the jury. Thus the most serious cases are dealt with by the *cour d'assises* where the three judges retire together with nine jurors and the decision is taken on a majority secret ballot – in which a conviction requires eight votes. The

French procedure then (of which this is only the briefest sketch) is very different to the English criminal system – although there are rather more similarities with the Scottish system.

When the parliaments of Scotland and England were united it was a condition of the Treaty of Union that Scots law should retain its separate identity. It now stands half way between the continental and the English system. On the one hand Scottish law has long historical associations with France and up to the eighteenth century Scottish law students obtained their legal training by attending French universities like Paris, Bourges and Orleans while the works of French jurists could be quoted as authority in Scottish courts. The signs of this connection still survive. A Scottish barrister is an advocate: the equivalent of the French *avocat*. The French public prosecutor is called a *procureur* corresponding to the procurator fiscal in Scotland. It is the procurator fiscal who is responsible for the investigation of all criminal offences in his district. He has the power to issue instructions to the police and it is his decision whether criminal proceedings should be taken. On the other hand the Scottish trial procedure is accusatorial not inquisitorial. At a criminal trial the evidence is placed before the court by the prosecution and defence and tested by cross-examination. It is for the parties to the case to decide what evidence they will produce and it is not part of the job of the judge to act as inquisitor or to call for new evidence. He may clear up questions which are still in doubt but essentially his role is to 'preside at a forensic contest between two parties'.[6]

In England, the system is again different. In the words of Lord Gardiner, a former Lord Chancellor:

> Except in the comparatively rare cases undertaken by the Director of Public Prosecutions or a government department or a private citizen the police investigate cases reported to them, interrogate suspects, decide whether or not to prosecute and if so, whom and on what charges, interview witnesses, select all evidence and are responsible for the prosecution.[7]

On the face of it then it might appear that the English police had less to complain of than some other European forces. Indeed the point of Lord Gardiner's words was to demonstrate the case of *Justice* that the English system offends against the principle that the prosecution process should be (and seen to be) independent,

132

impartial and fair. However, the case of the critics of the English system centres not on the relative simplicity of the process whereby the police can decide to prosecute but on the difficulty in obtaining convictions once the prosecution decision has been taken. All too often, it is claimed, the guilty can escape conviction because of the elaborate protection given to an accused person. Thus under the English procedure a suspect can remain silent throughout not only the police investigation but also his trial without the judge at the end of the trial or the prosecuting counsel being able to comment on this silence to the jury. Again the English procedure requires that the policeman should administer a caution to a suspect once he has decided to charge him, warning the suspect that he need not make a statement but if he does it can be used at any subsequent trial. The police criticism here is that when the trial takes place the issue becomes not whether the accused made the statement but whether the policeman administered the caution at the correct time. For although these rules – part of the Judges Rules laid down to guide the police in questioning – do not have the force of law the trial judge may (and usually will) refuse to admit a statement if the rules here have been ignored.

The most comprehensive criticism of the English system has come from Sir Robert Mark. Mark's case is that historically the existence of extreme punishments for a wide range of offences led to extreme safeguards in trial procedure. Yet as the punishments (like hanging and flogging) have been abolished – the safeguards have remained untouched. The result is that today:

A suspected or accused person is still able to play an entirely negative part in the investigation and trial in all but exceptional circumstances. He is not required to answer questions. He must be cautioned against self incrimination. He need not enter the witness box. His previous bad character must not ordinarily be mentioned at his trial. He is not required to disclose his defence before his trial and thus can – and frequently does – adduce false evidence which the prosecution does not have the opportunity to disprove.[8]

According to Mark the men most able to take advantage of such protection are not the unintelligent and weak criminal but the professional criminal from whom the public is most at risk. Many of these, he says, are acquitted and he points to an acquittal rate of between forty and fifty per cent (of those who plead not guilty) as adding statistical strength to his case.

Needless to say Mark's views are widely challenged. Rival statistics have been produced to show that, for example, one third of acquittals result from the direction of a judge that the case is too weak to continue. In other words it is suggested that the police in England prosecute too readily as compared to say France or Germany where proportionately less prosecutions are brought but where conviction rates are higher. Nor do all policemen agree with Mark. One senior detective with thirty years experience was critical of some lawyers:

> Legal aid has transformed the prosperity of the bar. Dock briefs used to be handed out for the unsuccessful and the down and almost out. I remember one barrister who had a room in Rowton House. But now the spread of legal aid has virtually eliminated the unsuccessful. One result is that there are quite obvious cases where the man is guilty. The trial is prolonged for three or four days.

His main criticism, however, was of 'sharp shooters' among solicitors:

> A number of them set out deliberately on a policy of attacking the police. They are always liable to play a dirty trick. There are also some who are not unwilling to arrange a defence. It is quite obvious that the defence was never worked out by the poor individual standing on trial.

Yet for all his reservations about the behaviour of lawyers the same detective said:

> I have never found any difficulty with the Judges Rules. I have been challenged all right but I have always won the day.

An even more fundamental defence has been put by Radzinowicz. Although recognizing 'a dark figure of abuse of criminal justice' his view is that:

> It is precisely when public feeling mounts most strongly against crime and criminals that safeguards are most needed. The criminal law should be the Magna Carta not only of those accused of crime but of all of us.

Yet for all the criticism heaped upon him and his theories Mark can point to one arguably conclusive piece of supporting evidence based not upon statistics but common sense and produced not by policemen but by lawyers – the 1972 report of the Criminal Law Revision Committee.[9] The committee, which included half a dozen judges as well as distinguished academics like Professor Glanville Williams accepted that the public now faced a threat from the professional criminal:

> There is now a large and increasing class of sophisticated professional criminals who are not only highly skilful in organising their crimes and in the steps they take to avoid detection but are well aware of their legal rights and use every possible means to avoid conviction if caught.

According to the committee times had also changed in other ways. Many nineteenth-century trials were conducted at break-neck speed – often no more than a few minutes – and legal representation was far less common. Legal aid was now usually available and no one could accuse the courts of indecent haste. Without then going to the European practice of making all relevant evidence admissible the committee sought to extend 'admissibility as far as is possible without the risk of injustice to the accused.' In a detailed series of proposals to this end they proposed that a jury should be able to draw whatever inferences are reasonable from the failure of the accused, when interrogated, to mention a defence which he puts forward at his trial, and following this first proposal, that the caution should be changed to warn the suspect that if he holds his defence back until his trial then: 'Your evidence may be less likely to be believed and this may have a bad effect on your case in general.'

So far, however, not even the weight of the Criminal Law Revision Committee has forced a change in the English law. The reason seems to be that in England (as in other European countries) the argument tends swiftly to polarise. Even those who propose modest changes to prevent the escape of the guilty are categorized as being intent upon reducing the fairness of the trial itself. Yet as the Criminal Law Revision Committee pointed out, fairness:

> means or ought to mean, that the law should be such as will secure as far as possible that the result of the trial is the right one. That is to say, the accused should be convicted if the

evidence proves beyond reasonable doubt that he is guilty, but otherwise not. We stress this . . . because fairness seems often to be thought of as something which is due to the defence only.

It is, of course, an acutely difficult area. Governments in democracies like to be portrayed as defending freedom rather than attacked for limiting it. Yet governments must also beware of winning an easy popularity while turning a blind eye to developments in crime. In the end they will not be thanked if as the result of their inaction the professional criminal continues to prosper.

10

Full Circle?

Every major police force has its intelligence branch. The British have the Special Branch; the French the *Renseignements Généraux;* and the Germans use a section of the *Bundeskriminalamt.* Thus in each country the police gathers information on at least some of the public: a function which can very easily lead them into major controversy. Police intelligence depends heavily upon informers, and involves the use of methods like telephone tapping. Information will be gathered on entirely innocent men and women, and surveillance will be kept on groups who are exercising normal political rights. Historically, of course, it is this area which has been most sensitive of all in relations between police and public and in Britain the fear of police spies seriously delayed the introduction of an organized police. While France – more than one and a half centuries after Fouché – continues to throw-up cases which, if nothing else, demonstrate that the gathering of intelligence remains a highly sensitive area of police work. Such a case was the affair of the satirical weekly *Le Canard Enchaîné* at the end of 1973.

The story began on the night of 3 December when the magazine's manager together with one of the principal cartoonists happened to be passing the magazine's new, but as yet unoccupied, offices. Attracted by lights on the third floor of the building the two entered only to find three men in overalls, accompanied by two civilians, working in the corner of one room. Holes had been drilled in the walls and floorboards and two microphones were among the workmens' equipment. When challenged one of the workmen replied that he had 'come for the central heating' – which had been completely fitted three days previously. Not surprisingly dissatisfied with this explanation the manager left to alert his editor. By the time the editor reached the scene the workmen had gone –

but the row had only just begun. Under banner head-lines *Water-gate au Canard* and *Oh Marcellin. Quelle Watergaffe* (Raymond Marcellin was the Minister of the Interior), the *Canard* went to work.

For the French Government the affair could not have come at a worse time. Already battered by a number of embarrassing domestic rows, the break-in appeared to be a rather crude attempt to counter the efforts of *Le Canard Enchaîné* which had already published a claimed facsimile of the income tax returns of Jacques Chaban-Delmas, the then Prime Minister, and had just turned its attention to electronic espionage. In June the magazine had published another facsimile of a *police* transcript of a telephone conversation between one of its reporters and a government official which prompted a parliamentary committee to look into the whole practice of telephone tapping. The result of this was a finding that the security authorities were tapping up to five thousand telephones a day. Nor was there very much doubt (even initially) that the break-in had been carried out by one of France's two main intelligence agencies – the *Direction de la Surveillance du Territoire* (DST)

DST is broadly equivalent to MI5 and its major role is to counter subversion of the state which originates abroad: it would for example, act against foreign intelligence agencies working in France. Unlike Britain, however, the men who work for it come from the police. They are skimmed off at an early stage in their career and never return to police service. Theoretically the division between DST and the *Renseignements Généraux* (RG) is simple. While the DST counters espionage from outside the country the RG guards against internal subversion. Again staffed by policemen the RG goes much further than most European countries would allow in, for example, checking on the activities of political parties, and reporting back on public feeling throughout the country. The RG, for example, correctly predicted the 1975 French Presidential elections. Yet simple as the division might appear the question arose in the early Seventies of which of the security organizations should deal with terrorism. Both organizations would make reasonable claim for the job but in the end the French Government gave the major responsibility to the DST. One theory is that – put out by this decision – it was the RG who tipped off the *Canard Enchaîné* staff about the efforts of their rivals and thus the Government were presented with a major political row because of the jealousies between agencies. Whether true or not the case certainly shows the dangers both to the public and to governments when intelligence gathering gets out of hand.

Yet although the affair of the *Canard Enchainé* certainly provides ample argument against inadequately controlled intelligence organizations it hardly disposes of the main question of whether such organizations are necessary for protecting the state. Here there is no question of the views of European governments. The strength of police intelligence forces are tending to rise and the reason for the rise is the extent and nature of the terrorist threat. Behind almost all terrorist movements is a political object. Mostly the public will reject the means although some may have sympathy with the political aim. But there are others still who supporting the political aim will accept or acquiesce in the means. It is here that the danger comes. In Ulster support is given to terrorists by men and women who would never fire a shot or plant a bomb – and Ulster is not alone. Even a country as prosperous and outwardly stable as West Germany can provide unexpected reservoirs of public support for terrorists.

The Red Army Faction (*Rote Armee Fraktion*) has always been better known by the names of two of its original leaders as the Baader-Meinhof gang. Its origins lay in the extreme left wing groups which flourished in Germany in the late Sixties and with the failure of violent demonstration the group turned to direct action. The aim remained to topple the established system and again the hope was that this would be helped by an over reaction from police and courts. Thus when the RAF turned to crime they initially chose crimes which not only provided resources but also could attract some public sympathy for them. One of their most dramatic early actions was in Berlin in September 1970 when the group succeeded in carrying out three simultaneous bank robberies and it was these raids which were to set the pattern. Throughout 1971 and into 1972 the bank robberies continued in cities and towns throughout West Germany. For the terrorists the banks made an ideal target. When an old lady is robbed of her savings there is public outrage but when a bank is robbed there is not the same identifiable loss and public sympathy can all too easily go to the robber. The RAF tried to exploit this sympathy by explaining to the public that the money in the banks had been returned to its rightful owners, the people. The group were doing no more than expropriating the proceeds of capitalism.

In May 1972 a new phase of the campaign began. On 11 May a bomb was placed at the headquarters of the 5th United States Air Force in Frankfurt killing an American colonel and injuring over fifty others. The next day bombs went off at the police headquarters at Augsburg and the headquarters of the *Landeskriminalamt* in Munich. On 15 May an assassination attempt was made on the judge in charge of the investigations into the group itself. On 19 May bombs damaged the Axel Springer building in Hamburg and on 24 May three Americans were killed by another bomb planted at the headquarters of the United States forces at Heidelberg. For the terrorists it was a decisive change of tactics.

Up to this point much public sympathy had been on the side of the RAF. Press comment was frequently critical of 'the hysteria' of the police and government and the public mood was well described by the BBC correspondent Ian McDougall in a despatch in March 1971:

> When a bus driver's seven year old son was recently kidnapped from a village near Bonn, the general bewilderment as to the motive was immediately dispersed, and the sense of outrage to a large extent dispelled, by the statement that the *intended* victim had been the son of the American consul. If its political people seem to understand it: it's still wrong but there's a redeeming feature of an ideological nature.[1]

Other public support went far beyond general sympathy. One of the mysteries surrounding the group was how they managed to lie low so sucessfully between actions. The reason became apparent after one or two of the group had been caught and put on trial. The group, who were predominantly drawn from the middle class, were helped by others from the middle class. University professors, social workers and journalists offered them shelter in their own homes or lent them flats and it was only when the group turned to bombs that this support began to be withdrawn. Thus it was only at the stage when the public felt themselves at risk or were sufficiently appalled by what was happening that the police were given full support.

The assumption then that the illegal and violent means of the urban terrorist will automatically mean public support for the police should not be too easily accepted – even in a developed community like West Europe. If the terrorist goes to the extent of endangering the public generally and indiscriminately – as with the planting of bombs – then the assumption probably holds good. Although even then there can be a tiny minority ready to protect even the most extreme terrorist. But what is worse is that there is a public tolerance of violence which appears to be for political ends. This is not to say that such violence will win mass support but it can win enough to make the police job infinitely more difficult. Thus the police have a clear operational need for intelligence which is probably greater than at any time in its history. Those who argue against the existence of police intelligence organizations must explain how otherwise they believe that the public can be protected from groups who have expressly rejected the methods of the democratic state.

But it is not just the terrorist who has produced a need for intelligence. As crime has become more organized police forces have been forced to devise new methods both nationally and internationally to combat it. An example of the national method is the criminal intelligence index at Scotland Yard which now goes significantly further than a simple (if massive) collection of criminal records, photographs and fingerprints. In addition there are two specialized indices. The first contains the details of about 250 'target criminals'. According to one senior policeman:

These would include the top class robbers. We wouldn't have details of the man who sticks a note over the counter saying 'I've got a gun – hand over £200.' But it would include the teams who operate masked and armed with shotguns. The first index then would put together the disjointed reports of different officers on these men – their associates, their habits, where they eat and drink, the cars they use.

The second index contains details of the men and women who are known to be active criminals and again the effort is made to build up a picture which can be invaluable to the investigating detective. The same senior officer said:

These are the second division criminals. They are the men and women known to be actively participating in crime. In London they may number about ten thousand. So its not just a question of putting everyone else in the second index. They will include burglars, the men who carry out the smaller kind of robberies, some receivers. It wouldn't include the man who steals from a motor car.

At the international level Interpol (the International Criminal Police Organization) keeps detailed records of around seven hundred thousand criminals at its headquarters in the fashionable Paris suburb of St Cloud. Interpol exists essentially as a channel for information – 'a glorified wireless station' as one senior detective irreverently put it. Information comes in from police forces around the world and is relayed onwards either automatically or on demand. Thus the section which deals with counterfeit currency keeps records on all known international 'pushers' and will either respond to an inquiry made through one of the national bureaux or pass on information that, for example, the pusher has moved to another country. A further section deals with fraud and apart from responding to requests for information will send out general circulation to police forces. One policeman seconded to Interpol said: 'They may give information about the Englishman who doesn't pay his hotel bills. The Belgian who poses as a football star or a charity organiser or the Spaniard who speaks eleven languages.' While in addition Interpol circulates notifications of criminals wanted by various national police forces. What, however, Interpol is much more reluctant to do is to get involved in so-called 'political crime'. Although their attitude to terrorism has changed in the last few years (terrorism is now regarded as largely criminal) Interpol is not as effective in this area as in tackling undisputed international crime. Clearly there are difficulties for Interpol – which has a charter which excludes 'political crime' and a breadth of membership which takes in right and left and Israeli and Arab. Nevertheless for Europe it is a potential chink in the defences.

Interpol's reluctance to become involved in 'political crime', however, is the exception to the trend. For the fact is that rather than diminish over the years the importance of intelligence gathering has increased. Countries like Britain which have been most suspicious of such operations – the Special Branch was established half a century after the formation of the police itself – recognize the importance of good intelligence in the same way as countries like France who have always put emphasis on it. In Britain there has been an unmistakable change of attitude. At the beginning of the nineteenth century both public and politicians rejected the use of 'police-spies'. Today the use of informers by the police is far more accepted – albeit as a necessary evil. As Lord Parker, the Lord Chief Justice, remarked in 1974:

In these days of terrorism the police have to be entitled to use the effective weapon of infiltration. In other words it has to be accepted today – if ever the contrary was ever considered – that it is a perfectly lawful police weapon in appropriate cases.[2]

What evidence there is suggests that this view is shared by the majority of the public: the savagery and violence of the IRA has seen to that. But what is also true of Britain today is that the purpose of intelligence gathering is totally different from that of say eighteenth- and nineteenth-century France. The aim is to counter a well identified danger. Dossiers are not being kept for their own sake but, in the final analysis, to help prevent the public being killed and injured by the terrorist or robbed and burgled by the more conventional criminal. The position then is not one of full circle but realistic response to an undoubted threat to the public and the state.

Yet even given that threat a wise government still insists that there must be checks on the abuse of power. If damaging errors – like the *Canard Enchainé* affair – are to be avoided then close government control over the intelligence agencies is necessary. This, it should be emphasised, is not just to save the government itself from embarrassment but to avoid the public losing confidence in this most easily criticized part of police work. As *The Times* put it in a leading article:

If the public on the side of the law comes to feel that its cause is being sustained to a large extent by methods that are lawless it may become confused and weary of the effort. If there is allowed to come into being a secret police force, operating according to no rules, or to rules of its own devising, and protected from public scrutiny and control, no one is safe and no one can be easy in his mind.[3]

Checks, however, are difficult because of the nature of the work. A case in point is the informer who has penetrated a terrorist group. Clearly such an informer must show some enthusiasm for the cause he is supposed to be supporting otherwise he will soon be detected. Equally he should not act as an *agent provocateur* causing offences to be carried out which otherwise would not have been committed at all. The difficulties and dangers of such operations were well shown in the case of Kenneth Joseph Lennon in 1974.

Lennon was a police informer who had provided an account of

Irish Republican extremists operating in the Luton area. As the result of the information he provided three men were arrested for conspiring to commit an armed robbery and at their trial were each sentenced to ten years imprisonment. The Special Branch encouraged him to maintain close contacts with one Irishman in particular, Patrick O'Brien, but plans went seriously wrong when both were arrested in Birmingham. Ultimately both men stood trial for conspiring to effect an escape from Winson Green prison but whereas O'Brien was convicted Lennon was acquitted and set free. Returning to London he made his way to the offices of the National Council for Civil Liberties where he made a statement that he had been forced into working for the Special Branch and to act as an *agent provocateur*. Arrangements were made for him to return to the NCCL offices to complete and sign his statements. However, three days later he was found dead in a ditch near a Surrey town having been shot. In fact a subsequent inquiry found that Lennon had volunteered to work for the Special Branch – his motive being money – and that there was no evidence of his having acted as an *agent provocateur*. Yet what is significant about the Lennon case was that, tangled and delicate as it was, elaborate checks took place to ensure that power had not been abused.

The immediate result of the Lennon murder was an inquiry carried out for the Home Secretary by the Deputy Commissioner of the Metropolitan Police. This in itself formed the basis of a statement in the Commons by the Home Secretary, Roy Jenkins, and later the Commissioner's report was published – in spite of the fact that it contained a detailed picture of Special Branch operations.[4] While in the Court of Appeal two of the three men convicted on Lennon's information of conspiring to commit armed robbery sought leave to appeal against conviction.

In other words the position was again established that the Home Secretary is accountable to Parliament for the activities of the police including the Special Branch; while Special Branch officers are themselves accountable to the courts (and indeed the police complaints procedure) for their actions. The police intelligence branch is not therefore a law to itself but operates subject to two fundamental checks – the responsibility of the controlling minister to an elected assembly and the check of the law. To those outright opponents of intelligence-gathering such checks will doubtless seem inadequate. For those however who accept that it is a necessary part of police work – and never more than today – such checks offer assurance that at the same time that the public interest is maintained the individual's interest will be protected.

Private Security

On the face of it another example of where Europe (and most of all Britain) has gone full circle is on the role of non-police security organizations. The formation of the police in Britain recognized one central fact: that no longer could the public be protected without the establishment of an organized police. The role of the police was emphatically preventive: the detection of criminals and the punishment of offenders came lower down the initial scale of priorities. As the first orders issued to the Metropolitan Police put it: 'It should be understood at the outset that the principal object to be attained is the prevention of crime. To this great end every effort of the police is to be directed.'

Today, however, all European forces are being forced to give more priority to detecting crime, preserving public order and handling emergencies and correspondingly less to work on preventing crime. One example makes the point. In the 1950s and into the early 1960s the police in Britain were still able to provide police escort services for cash in transit. But by the 1960s the rise in criminal attacks on cash being transported produced a demand for police protection which forces were unable to provide. The result was that the 1960s and the 1970s saw the development of cash in transit services by private companies.

Already such companies offered guard services to protect factories and offices, but cash in transit brought them before many of the public for the first time. Some of the public clearly did not like what they saw. In countries like France and Belgium security guards who carry money are armed; while in Britain some companies equip their men with staves as a weapon of defence. Another expressed fear was that the private companies were becoming too powerful. The biggest company in Britain, Securicor, rivals in size the Metropolitan Police, while other giants include Securitas (a company formed in Sweden which is the biggest in Europe)* and several American companies like Brinks with European subsidiaries. Yet loud as the voices have sometimes been against

---

* The author acts as adviser to Group Four: the British subsidiary of Securitas.

private security remarkably little attention has been given to policy towards them. Most governments inside the Common Market have taken little interest in the development of the industry and have paid little attention to the dangers which have accompanied the growth – dangers which come not from the big companies who have most to lose if things go wrong but from small companies who are not able to provide the required level of service. In Britain the true irony is that although it took fifty years to overcome public fears of an organized police anyone can start a security company. There are no formalities and no checks. Criminals can and do enter the industry.

Just how long the British system (if such it can be called) can survive without a major scandal is a matter of speculation. But not all countries inside the Common Market are so content to leave the industry unchecked. In Belgium, for example, licences are issued to security companies, which are subject to renewal after two years. Each company has to provide a list of shareholders – to prevent criminals controlling security companies – while staff are officially checked as free from criminal conviction. This last check operates by placing the responsibility upon the man applying for a job with a security company to obtain a certificate from the police that he has no criminal record. The Belgian example would be a good one for Britain to follow. For only those who believe that crime will radically diminish over the next few years can seriously believe that private security companies will fade away. Nor given the already enormous demands on police manpower can it seriously be argued that the police can take over the security companies' role. Certainly it is true that attention should be given to the dividing line between what is work for policemen and security men: a rough guide mark is that only policemen should do the jobs which bring them into face-to-face contact with the public like demonstrations. Nevertheless when it comes to jobs like standing guard on factories or carrying cash for banks and supermarkets the security companies have a valuable role to play. The responsibility of governments is to ensure that certain minimum standards are observed by such companies.

11

Morals and the Law

The police are not arbiters upon morals. They do not have to decide whether pornography corrupts; whether prostitution degrades; or whether the individual has the right to destroy himself by drugs. Their area of decision is limited and theoretically simple. As one London policeman put it: 'I am not concerned with morals at all. That is the job of the legislature. I am only concerned with whether it is lawful or not. Supposing it is unlawful what must I do to discharge the burden of proof? Supposing I do discharge the burden of proof what will be the reaction of the courts?'

Unfortunately for the police, however, legislatures have often been uncertain what they intended; the laws themselves are frequently ill-defined; and the reactions of the courts can be inconsistent and unpredictable. The result is that all too often in practice the police are left to sort out the muddle as best they can and frequently carry the blame for the deficiencies in the law enforcement process itself.

From one side they are attacked for intervening on questions which concern no one but the individual – even though one law may require that they should intervene. While from the opposite extreme they are criticized for not intervening – even though another law may make it unlikely that they will secure a conviction. The police then run the risk of losing both ways. Action can bring the charge that they have become moral censors; inaction can produce the scarcely veiled hint that they have been bought off. In itself this produces an obvious dilemma for the police but there is an additional question which is even more fundamental. Should the police enforce laws when a substantial body of opinion believes the restrictions to be unnecessary? For if they do will it not inevitably lead them into head on conflict with the public?

These problems have faced most European countries and over the last ten years the classic (if that is the right word) battleground has been pornography. Most people know what they mean by pornography but finding a generally acceptable definition has defeated every legislature. The English have at least tried for precision and most prosecutions are brought on the grounds of obscenity.[1] The law covers books, films, magazines, records, photographs and cards and the test is whether the total effect is a tendency 'to deprave and corrupt' the user. The producer, however, can justify the obscene by showing that it is for the 'public good' on the ground that it is in the interests of science, literature, art or learning or of other objects of general concern and can call a string of expert witnesses to support him. Even with this limitation the English definition may seem pretty vague but other European countries have left the legal test even more in the air. In Holland, for example, the Dutch penal law forbids the production, distribution or display of any article which offends 'public morality'. While in Denmark the law which covered books up to 1967 simply prohibited the production and distribution of 'obscene publications' and left the police and the courts to work it out for themselves. It was the failure of this Danish law which has had the most profound effect in Europe.

In 1964 *Fanny Hill*, John Cleland's detailed account of life in an eighteenth-century London brothel, went on trial in both London and Copenhagen. In London the Chief Metropolitan Magistrate of Bow Street ordered 170 copies of the book to be destroyed but in Copenhagen *Fanny Hill* fared considerably better. Although six years earlier an English edition of the book had been convicted as obscene the Danish Supreme Court this time acquitted the two publishers who had prepared a new Danish edition. The whole law was immediately thrown into confusion. As one policeman serving in Copenhagen at the time said 'If *Fanny Hill* was not pornographic it was difficult to think off hand of any other writings which the court would consider were.' Responding to the new situation the Minister of Justice set up a committee to examine the whole area of pornography and it was following their recommendation that in 1967 the Danish Parliament repealed all the laws on pornographic writing. Two years later Parliament effectively finished the job and repealed the remaining restrictions covering pornographic pictures – although here they attempted to stop sales to children under sixteen.

The 'Danish experiment', involving the almost total removal of all legal controls over pornography, had begun.

Today the Danes proclaim themselves well satisfied with the results. The prevailing view among both government officials and senior policemen is that the policy change has 'de-dramatized' pornography. Sales of pornographic books and pictures have dropped dramatically since the peaks reached when the law was about to be changed. Traders who turned their newspaper and tobacco shops into 'porn shops' have now changed them back again. Sex magazines have fallen on hard times and the cinemas are back to John Wayne and Barbara Streisand. The Danish case is that the Danes themselves have become satiated with pornography and that demand fell away naturally once the novelty of legally available pornography wore off. One senior policeman summarized the case: 'The change was not intended to encourage pornography – far from it. The whole philosophy was that if you liberalised the law then people would lose interest.'

The police say that the big demand now comes from tourists. Sex shops are confined largely to the tourist centre of Copenhagen; the cinemas which still show pornographic films change their repertoire once the summer season ends; and even the clubs offering 'live shows' (usually simulated sex on stage) now play largely to foreign visitors. It was the live shows which so shocked Lord Longford when he took his committee to Denmark in 1971 but since then the situation has changed. The number of clubs has reduced from a peak of one hundred and twenty to around half a dozen. 'The interest in live shows in this country is over', said the head of the police club section. 'All the people we meet now are tourists.' Here the police do still have an interest. Although the Danes themselves can belong to clubs producing live shows the Ministry of Justice has directed the police to take action against clubs simply bringing in tourists off the street. But restrictions in Denmark are very much the exception. The general rule is that anything goes and the Danish public can take it or leave it.

In 1973 Germany followed very much the same course. In spite of fierce opposition from the churches and the Christian Democrats most restrictions on the sale of pornography were lifted. The reasoning behind the change was put by an official of the Ministry of the Interior in Bonn: 'We thought it was not the task of the state to prevent people from buying pornography. This is

149

their own decision. It is a moral decision and not a decision for us.'

The result is that today pornography can be bought in bookshops (although not legally by those under eighteen) and the Germans hope that demand will peak out and then fall. As a portent they point to the reduction in cinemas showing pornographic films. 'The boom is over,' said the same official. 'People have seen enough.'

In Holland the progression has been technically different but very much to the same effect. The law itself, which forbids publications that offend public morality and threatens maximum sentences of a year's imprisonment, is still on the statute book. But a policy decision by the public prosecutors have made it clear to the police that they will take action only in certain situations. They will try to protect children and they will prosecute pornography on public display which, for example, depicts sadism or sex with animals. For the rest the authorities turn a blind eye. The law has thus been effectively changed by administrative decision and it seems likely that it will soon be changed in substance as well.

There seems little doubt then that once one country relaxes its laws it has a domino effect on other countries. The example is held up as showing a way forward. It is eagerly studied not only by the campaigners against all forms of censorship but often by the authorities in enforcing the law. But the effect is not only persuasive. Once a country legalizes, for example, the reading of pornography it also legalizes its production. In Europe with its open borders this is important for it means that a legal production centre has been set up cheek by jowl to nations where pornography is still illegal. For the producer there is the magnet of a nearby export market where prices are high and where the normal criminal risk has been substantially reduced. He still faces the problem of getting his products into the target country but his home base remains secure, legal and above board. In Denmark these opportunities have been grasped eagerly.

The Danish producers of pornography now get the bulk of their profits from the export trade chiefly to Britain and the United States but also to countries like Italy and Spain. In actually exporting the pornography they run a risk only if they send it by post but the risk is hardly enormous. Although Denmark remains party to an international agreement which prohibits the sending of pornography by post the police are not over-active in trying to detect it. 'We only take action if we have a complaint from abroad', said one of the most senior policemen in Copenhagen. Even then action is likely to be ineffective. As domestic production is legal the police maintain no checks on producers and therefore build up no intelligence on the exporters. In effect the only threat to the Danish producers comes from the police and customs officials in the unwilling importing nations. Some is detected but much manages to get through by car, post or even the big containers bringing in hermogenically sealed Danish bacon. Thus the net effect of the Danish experiment on a country like England is to make the law substantially more difficult to enforce.

On pornography England has moved against the European tide. The 1959 Obscene Publications Act is by far the most important law in this field but it is not the only weapon which can be used by the police. The 1953 Post Office Act prohibits the sending of 'indecent or obscene' articles by post and large numbers of postal packets, mainly from abroad, are destroyed each year. Action is also still taken under two early nineteenth-century acts – the 1824 Vagrancy Act and the 1829 Indecent Advertisements Act – which deals with public exhibition and prohibits the public display of any obscene print, picture, or other indecent exhibition. Far from these restrictions being scrapped it seemed that at one stage they would be extended when the Conservative Government in 1973 introduced a bill mainly aimed at preventing 'the public being unwillingly exposed to indecent material' on display in bookshop windows or advertised on cinema posters. The term 'indecent' was left undefined but the intention was made clear enough by the then Home Secretary, Robert Carr. 'I am concerned,' he said, 'with what I call the soft end of the pornographic spectrum, which really is indecency as distinct from what might be called the hard end, or obscenity, which is already covered by the obscenity laws.'[2] But the extension was not to be. The 1974 election caught the legislation in midstream and the new Labour Government quickly announced that it would not be re-introduced. The obscenity laws, however, remain intact – although some believe, and others fear, that England will in due course follow the European example.

In Europe the clinching argument which has persuaded governments to scrap their laws has been that public demand for pornography dooms to failure all efforts to prevent it. In other words it is claimed that law in this area is inherently unenforceable. There is here an obvious analogy. The same argument has led many European countries to give a reluctant stamp of approval to prostitution. In Amsterdam all efforts in the past to stamp out prostitution failed and the position today is, in the words of one Dutch policeman, that 'it is not legal but it is not illegal.' What this means in practice is that provided the prostitutes remain in the 'red light' area behind Dam Square they are allowed to operate openly and virtually without hindrance. Only if they leave their recognized limits do they risk running foul of the police. In Munich a similar arrangement confines prostitutes to a number of streets and to 'eros houses' which are in effect brothels where clients are able to make their choice in the foyer rather than in the street. There are regular police inspections and one view in the Munich police is that the city authorities should in effect run prostitution to prevent the exploitation of the girls by the pimps, who purr round the city in their white Mercedes sports cars. While in England itself the prostitute can now operate perfectly legally from her flat provided that she does not turn it into a brothel. In all three cases the motive force has been that prostitution cannot be prevented and that the only alternative is to allow it within defined limits. This is almost precisely the position with nations who have changed their pornography laws. Some limits remain – like the prohibition on sales to children and the sale of some kinds of pornography – but the bulk of the law has been abandoned as being beyond the capacity of the police and the courts to enforce.

There is no doubt that the English police share these enforcement difficulties. Much pornography is obvious enough; magazines, slides, and films depicting sadism, bestiality and lesbianism. Fifty years ago D. H. Lawrence wrote 'what is pornography to one man is the laughter of genius to another.' There is very little laughter in the deliberate crude pornography of the 1970s. Yet although these are the staple products of the pornography trade they are often ignored in the public discussion. The law – and the enforcement of it – tends to be judged by a handful of cases on the margin.

This point was recognized by Mr Peter Brodie in 1970 when he was assistant commissioner in charge of crime at Scotland Yard. In an internal memorandum Brodie revealed all too clearly the difficulties and fears of the police when he wrote:

It is clear that there is a level of pornography which is exceptionally delicate, where any police action will obviously attract much publicity, subsequent analysis and criticism. It is impossible to set out an exhaustive list but obvious examples are:

(a) Displays in recognised galleries and books expensively published.
(b) Works of alleged or real masters.
(c) Exhibitions of famous, infamous or notorious individuals.
(d) Films at private clubs and associations.

In any such case which is likely to be the source of more than average publicity it is necessary to establish and determine police action with proportionate care.

Brodie therefore ordered all cases in this class to be referred to him and added:

Police will not seek out such displays or exhibitions to discover possible obscenity offences. Only when the weight of complaints makes it necessary to determine what police action, if any, should be taken will we trouble ourselves with such matters. BEFORE ANY INQUIRIES are made, even of an exploratory nature, a report will be submitted for the information, consideration and directions of the Assistant Commissioner Crime.[3]

The instruction well reflects the caution with which the English police proceed. They tread carefully and rarely chance their arm. In most criminal cases the police prosecute at their own discretion. With obscenity they consider the scope for legal disagreement so great that they have effectively handed over the decision to the Director of Public Prosecutions. Thus in London the police gather the evidence but it is the Director who decides whether a prosecution is started. Some campaigners against pornography maintain that the English approach is too pussy-footing by half. However what they ignore is the very substantial success that the police have had in the last few years against the worst forms of pornography.

The traditional centre for pornography in England is the Soho district of London and it is here that the police's most dramatic success has come. Until 1972 action against pornography in Soho was largely in the hands of the Obscene Publications Squad of the Metropolitan Police based at Scotland Yard. In 1972 the squad was reorganized and their effort supplemented by a small five man unit based in Soho itself. The result of this change was startling. In the six months following there were one hundred raids on 'porn shops' and altogether twenty thousand magazines and two thousand films were seized. With magazines fetching prices (even then) of £6 or £7 each and a ten minute film retailing at between £20 and £30 the loss for the shop owners was substantial. The immediate effect was that the shops reduced their stocks to one or two days' supplies and kept their major reserves outside Soho. But even this was not enough to save them. The raids continued and the owners were now beginning to appear in court. Although some escaped with relatively low fines others were fined heavily and still others were sent to prison. Indeed had it not been for the anomaly in the obscenity laws which fails to give the police the right of arrest even more would have appeared in court. As it was some of the pornography traders were able to go into hiding and never answered the court summons. Meanwhile at Scotland Yard the police had moved onto the next stage and were trying to cut off the supplies at source by bringing to court the English producers and suppliers of pornography.

Today the kind of hard pornography which is thrust at the public in Copenhagen and Amsterdam is simply not on display in Soho. It would be too much to claim that it cannot be obtained but certainly it has been made appreciably more difficult than it was only a few years ago. The most common method of supply is now by mail-order. Typically the pornography is produced in Scandinavia and the orders are processed in 'post-box' offices outside Britain – often in Amsterdam. The pornography is then imported in bulk and distributed from inside Britain. Yet even here customs officers are having increasing success and the volume of imported pornography has been reduced. According to one senior policeman in London the net result of action by police and customs is that the volume of imported pornography now available in Britain has been reduced to 'about one quarter of what was available in 1972.'

In effect then the police in England have shown that a middle way is possible. This does not involve tying down vast numbers of policemen (there are a dozen policemen in Scotland Yard's obscene publications squad) nor blundering unprepared and without consistent legal policy into an obvious area of public controversy. But it does prevent Parliament from feeling that it has no option but to change the law. It allows Parliament to consider the case for change on its merits. For there are very real dangers for any European country to accept the case that a law is unenforceable simply because there are admitted difficulties in enforcing it. There are other areas besides pornography – and prostitution – where there is an actual or potential public demand and where there are determined groups who would like nothing better than to sweep away the legal restrictions on the pretext that they have become unenforceable. An outstanding example of just such a campaign came in England in the 1960s.

When the 1960 Betting and Gaming Act went through Parliament Home Office ministers were specific about their aims. They conceded that the law against street betting had become unworkable and they proposed that legal betting shops should be allowed to cater for the undoubted public demand. They were equally specific about gaming which had no mass following and was chiefly confined to the Mayfair party belt. 'The Government do not wish to see casinos established,' said the Home Office minister handling the bill. 'If anything further can be added to the bill to make it more certain it will be considered.' The aim was clear enough. Yet by the middle of the Sixties a small empire of gaming clubs and casinos had been established and by the end of the decade they had become legal.

The attempts to defeat the purpose of Parliament began as soon as the act became law. Clubs offering *chemin de fer* and roulette sprouted up and they were certainly not to be put off by convictions before magistrates' courts. Almost invariably they appealed to a higher court and, although they usually lost, they succeeded in buying time while their appeals were pending. Once the appeals were finally rejected they quickly returned to the fray with new variations of the games which they claimed met all legal objections and the whole process started again. By 1966 the Metropolitan Police in London had become so heartily sick of the whole business that a new policy directive was issued. This was that: 'In view of the uncertainty of the law, the expense and manpower involved in keeping gaming observations in such clubs is not justified unless there are complaints of cheating or reason to suppose that a particular club has become a haunt of criminals.'[4] Thus the police would check whether a club was swindling the players and it would gather intelligence if it became a regular meeting place for criminals but in 1966 Scotland Yard gave up its attempts to enforce the law itself which had been intended to forbid gaming,

Views still differ on whether the Metropolitan Police were correct in this appreciation. Undoubtedly some lawyers believe that the act was so badly drafted that it could never have worked. Yet this hardly explains how a Superintendent in the tiny Southend force, who had read the act and then taken counsel's advice, was able to win two important gaming cases – although in one he was fought all the way to the House of Lords.[5] Nor does it explain the judgement of Lord Denning in the Court of Appeal when a former Labour MP, Raymond Blackburn, claimed that the Metropolitan Police were not meeting their duty to enforce the law. Lord Denning ended his judgement forcefully:

> This case has shown a deplorable state of affairs. The law has not been enforced as it should. The lawyers themselves are at least partly responsible. The niceties of drafting and refinements of interpretation have led to uncertainties in the law itself. This has discouraged the police from keeping observation and action; but it does not, I think, exempt them also from their share of the responsibility. The proprietors of gaming houses have taken advantage of the situation. By one device after another they have kept ahead of the law. As soon as one device has been held unlawful they have started another; but the day of reckoning is at hand. No longer will we tolerate these devices. The law must be sensibly interpreted so as to give effect to the intention of Parliament; and the police must see that it is enforced. The rule of law must prevail.[6]

In fact the day of reckoning never arrived. The Home Office took the view that it was too late to stamp gaming out and that if they tried there would be a real risk that it would go underground. Instead the Home Secretary, Roy Jenkins, decided he had no option but to legalize gaming and to control it within certain limits. The gaming clubs – with the aid of skilled legal advice – had won a speedy and significant victory. Another law had been officially declared unenforceable.

The important question for the future is whether the reasoning which has persuaded different European nations to legalize pornography, prostitution, betting and gaming will not next carry the day with drugs? Certainly there is no doubt that many of the same arguments can be made to apply. The public demand for soft drugs like cannabis exists and many young people consider the restrictions both medically unnecessary and an unwarranted interference with their freedom. There is also no doubt that the enforcement of the law presents the police with difficulties and a major area of potential friction with at least some of the public. Not all police raids on houses and clubs and not every search in the street will produce hashish. Each time the police get it wrong – as by the law of averages they must get it wrong – they leave themselves open to attack. Nor is there the slightest doubt that already these difficulties have led to a partial withdrawal of restrictions in some parts of Europe.

In most European countries the courts and the law distinguish between the penalties for pushers of drugs and the users. This is altogether sensible. There clearly is a distinction between a trader in drugs who does everything he can to create and exploit demand and a user who perhaps has taken the drug on only one or two occasions. Few would doubt that penalties should recognize this difference but several countries have pushed the distinction to the point of not prosecuting some drug users at all. In Holland prosecution policy was summed up by one legal expert: 'Dealers are always brought to court. Offences involving hard drugs are always brought to court. But if a boy is caught with a grain of hashish then the policy is not to bring him before a court.'

The Danes take this policy one step further. Penalties for the pusher have not only been maintained but increased so that he now faces a maximum sentence of up to ten years imprisonment. On the other hand the user – of either soft or hard drugs – will generally not be prosecuted. The Danes take the view that the way of dealing with the user is by treatment in the social welfare system rather than by appearance in the courts. Again it is possible to justify this course. By itself conviction in a court may do nothing to change the drug user whereas effective treatment does at least hold out this hope. But there are also dangers in a policy of non-prosecution.

Such a policy not only de-criminalizes the offence but also implicitly lays down the priorities for the police. Both Denmark and Holland deny that their policy amounts to an acceptance of drug taking. As one senior Amsterdam policeman said: 'With sufficient men you can have a policy. When you are under strength you can only have priorities.'

But what cannot be denied is that in this scale of priorities the detection of drug users in both countries comes low and sometimes very low. Certainly this is the view of many drug users. Both

Copenhagen and Amsterdam attract users from all over Europe. Nor is drug use confined to cannabis. Undisputed drugs of addiction like heroin and various other morphine based mixtures have also appeared in both countries. In August 1973 the Danish police had their first big seizure of imported heroin and the CID now fear that the Danish drugs problem is on the increase. In Amsterdam the authorities maintain an outward calm but this is not shared by all European observers. One of the most common fears expressed is that now Amsterdam has become established as a centre for cannabis increasing efforts will be made to establish and exploit a demand for heroin. At present it is true that neither Denmark nor Holland officially permit drug use but in both countries enforcement has been given a low priority and public demand has increased. It is at least a possibility that both countries could drift to a situation where the legislators felt that they had no option but to declare some forms of drug taking legal.

Of course it can be argued that this is precisely what should happen. But it is one thing for a law to be changed after debate and consideration of the evidence and quite another to slide to a break-down of the law because of partial or non-enforcement. The solution clearly lies with governments and legislatures. It is their responsibility to amend laws if they are deficient and it is their responsibility to scrap laws if they believe that they have become unnecessary. The trouble is that – in all countries – a policy of drift often rather suits the ministers and the legislators. Laws are often difficult to amend and action in the area of public morality risks controversy, unpopularity, and, worst of all, ridicule. The temptation to do nothing is great but from the police point of view this is worst of all. It puts them into a no-man's land where the courts are likely to reflect the official indecision and where the controversy unpopularity and ridicule centres on the police.

12

Traffic and the Law

The importance of relations between the police and the motorist was first recognized in Britain by a Home Office Committee of 1932. The Committee reported that before the First World War the day to day work of the police was concerned with the 'criminal class' and the most common offence was the offence of drunkenness. That had now all changed. Drunkenness had ceased to occupy a major part in the work of the police but the vast increase in motor traffic had brought the policeman into contact with all sections of the community – 'whereas before 1919 the constable had seldom to exercise authority over persons of a different social order from his own, now that is a common incident of his daily duty.'[1] A rather more modern statement of the same point came from the 1962 Royal Commission who observed that: 'The evidence before us showed that an important – according to some witnesses *the* most important – factor affecting relations between the police and the public today is the problem of enforcing the traffic laws. It is probably as motorists that ordinary men and women most often have dealings with the police.'[2]

The difficulty for the police is easy enough to understand. The public concerned – the motoring public – regard traffic law as basically different from the criminal law. Their typical response is that the police should spend less time on the motorist and more time catching 'real criminals.'

One comparison makes the point. The act of burglary is seen as undoubtedly criminal. The burglar presents a clear threat to the householder while the public do not feel themselves personally restricted by the law on burglary. It after all requires very little effort for the average person to avoid the consequences of the law. When it comes to motoring public attitudes change sharply. Here the motoring public do feel themselves directly threatened. Their view of the law tends to be that traffic regulations are so numerous that it would border on the miraculous if they were not breaking one of them. Inevitably attitudes to the police are coloured by these very different responses to the law. When it comes to burglary police success is applauded and the usual complaint is that the police are not doing enough to combat it. When it comes to traffic law the motorist often reacts angrily against the police-man who is enforcing it. As one Paris policeman said: 'The auto-matic response to a traffic ticket is to protest.'

Clearly, however, there is another side to the argument. In Britain six thousand five hundred people are killed each year in road accidents and a further seventy-five thousand seriously in-jured. In France the annual toll of deaths on the road is thirteen thousand; in Germany it is fourteen thousand five hundred; and in Italy nine thousand five hundred. Nor is there any doubt that it is human error which is responsible for the vast majority of these accidents. One British survey suggests that human error is a con-tributory factor in no less than ninety-five per cent of accidents. Governments then have placed on the police new obligations to en-force laws aimed at reducing the toll and, as the late Anthony Crosland put it, 'helping road users to behave more safely.'[3] Given the choice between police or no police it is fairly certain that the motoring public would plump for a police presence – at least in enforcing those laws which are seen to be most closely connected with their own safety. For although it may be true that most motor-ists consider most traffic laws non-criminal – it is equally true that there is some driving behaviour which they would characterize as criminal. Killing or injuring a pedestrian by dangerous driving would generally be regarded as criminal. By any objective standard drunken driving should also fall into the same category. Yet here public attitudes are notably equivocal.

The Drunken Driver

The basic facts concerning drunken driving are not in serious dispute. A whole series of studies have shown that drink (even in relatively small quantities) can impair a driver's performance. Thus in 1959 an experiment with a number of experienced Manchester bus drivers showed that some were willing after taking only two ounces of whisky to attempt to drive through a gap fourteen inches nar rower than their vehicles. Swedish tests in 1950 showed a marked deterioration in driving performance at levels as low as 40mg/100ml, and that finding was confirmed by a more recent survey which showed drivers unable to react fast enough to unforeseen hazards such as a figure appearing in the road in front of their cars. In the United States a 1963 survey found that drivers with a blood alcohol level of 150mg/100ml had a ten times higher than normal accident rate and drivers with 200mg/100ml had a twenty times higher rate.[4] While a recent survey of two thousand accidents in Britain carried out by the Transport Road Research Laboratory showed that a quarter of all accidents involved a drinking driver.

In terms of drink-related road accidents the toll is greatest among young drivers. In Britain half of all male deaths between fifteen and twenty-four are because of road accidents and the largest factor in these casualties is alcohol. While in addition to the young driver there are the alcoholics and near alcoholics who provide a special problem of their own. The most dangerous time for accidents is between 10.00 pm and 4.00 am and the risk of accidents increases sharply on Friday and Saturday nights: a finding confirmed by police in both Europe and the United States. There is then a clear link between road accidents and social activities – and it is this link which almost certainly explains the public tolerance of drunk driving. For although there is no question about the damage the drunk driver causes there remains a feeling of 'there but for the grace of God go I.'

Nevertheless today all West European nations do have laws based upon a prescribed maximum blood alcohol concentration. The two countries who introduced such tests earliest were Norway in 1937 and Sweden in 1941. They together with the Netherlands prescribe a limit of 50mg/100ml. Britain who only turned to this form of test in 1967 (and only then after strong opposition) has an 80mg limit – as too does Belgium, Denmark, France and the German Federal Republic. Most American states have a limit of 100mg while the Republic of Ireland has a limit of 120mg. But as we have seen time and time again what matters most is not the passing of law itself but how effectively it is enforced. Here practice varies widely. At one end of the scale is a country like Sweden where motorists can be stopped not only on suspicion that they have been drinking but also indiscriminately at a road block where every motorist is tested irrespective of whether there is any suspicion or not. The deterrent effect of such checks is clear enough : no driver can rely on his inherent skill or supposed ability to take liquor without effect to keep him out of trouble. At the opposite end of the scale is Britain which has been reluctant to give the police adequate powers to convict even the undoubtedly drunk driver – let alone give the police indiscriminate powers to stop guilty and innocent drivers alike.

The British law empowers a policeman to give a breath test 'if the constable has reasonable cause to suspect him of having alcohol in his body.'[5] However, a number of cases have strictly limited this power. One case established that the policeman must have arrested the driver according to the proper procedure and that if any of the arrest requirements were not met this invalidated a positive breathalyser finding. Another case established that the 'peculiar' driving behaviour of a driver did not necessarily create a reasonable suspicion that he had consumed alcohol : again the breathalyser finding was invalidated. Not surprisingly the effect has been that the police have been unquestionably cautious before conducting a test. One result of this has been that their 'success rate' as a proportion of tests conducted has been remarkably high even compared with a country like France which then had a similar law – as Table 4 shows.

Table 4[6]
BREATHALYSER TESTS (France and Britain)

1974	Tests	Positives	% Positive
France	1,093,000	60,000	5.5
Britain	143,000	83,000	58.00

(In France 600,000 tests were given as a matter of routine after minor traffic offences)

However, the other major result has been that the motorist has (rightly) come to the conclusion that his chances of being stopped are slight. Deaths in accidents where the driver was above the prescribed limit have increased and the initial effect of the drink-driving law has been dissipated.

Yet quite apart from the arguments on detail the British response to drunk-driving indicates a more general point – a failure to come to terms with the motor car (and indeed the lorry). At one end of the scale the police are given inadequate powers to deal with an offence which causes at least one in ten of all the deaths and

Table 5

PROCEEDINGS AT MAGISTRATES' COURTS, BY OFFENCE GROUP

ENGLAND AND WALES   Number of offences

Offence group	Offence type	1974	1975	1976
1	Causing death or bodily harm	671	709	721
2	Dangerous driving	13,167	13,184	12,817
3	Driving etc. after consuming alcohol or taking drugs	66,774	70,394	63,193
4	Careless driving etc.	160,567	163,374	165,118
5	Accident offences	39,020	42,281	43,733
6	Unauthorised taking or theft of motor vehicle	63,211	68,167	69,742
7	Driving licence related offences	120,403	121,621	125,626
8	Provisional licence offences	121,089	121,207	118,102
9	Vehicle insurance offences	174,787	181,564	188,454
10	Vehicle registration and excise licence offences	222,110	237,780	253,932
11	Work record and employment offences	22,773	22,550	19,835
12	Operator's licence offences	4,029	4,120	4,269
13	Vehicle test offences	103,114	106,419	111,818
14	Vehicle or part in dangerous or defective condition	193,539	193,097	195,704
15	Speed limit offences	311,660	313,519	365,364
16	Motorway offences (other than speeding)	10,195	10,834	13,568
17	Neglect of traffic directions	91,743	91,426	103,903
18	Neglect of pedestrian rights	35,258	32,765	33,198
19	Obstruction, waiting and parking offences	166,210	163,224	111,080
20	Lighting offences	116,028	95,690	97,303
21	Noise offences	11,828	11,550	11,711
22	Load offences	19,492	23,336	23,827
23	Trailer offences	820	666	745
24	Offences peculiar to motor cycles	10,564	11,902	12,204
25	Miscellaneous motoring offences	38,381	39,891	69,275
26	Other offences associated with motoring	1,931	741	869
	All offences	2,119,364	2,142,011	2,216,111
	Number of persons	1,339,622	1,355,769	1,418,265

163

injuries on the roads. At the other end of the scale British law requires that practically every offence concerned with a car or lorry should be dealt with in a court of law just like any other crime. Thus each year Magistrates' Courts deal with over two million motoring offences: two thirds of their work. As Table 5 shows these offences range from the unquestionably serious to violations which few would regard in the same way. In Britain little official thought has been given to separating the two groups – in spite of some persuasive arguments advanced by lawyers, academics and policemen. Changes have been confined largely to the law affecting the parked vehicle. Other countries have been more adventurous.

Major and Minor
Since 1969 the Germans have had a system based upon a judgement of the relative seriousness of different traffic offences. At the bottom end of the scale are offences which can be dealt with by either an on-the-spot fine or by a fixed penalty ticket. (The difference being that in the first case the fine is actually handed over: in the second it is collected through the post.) So a motorist who is speeding by no more than ten kilometres or fifteen kilometres above the limit will have the opportunity of discharging the penalty by paying a fixed fine. More serious traffic offences are dealt with at the next stage. A typical offence here would be speeding which was above the spot fine limit but where no injury resulted to another road user. A case here is dealt with administratively by an office coming under the charge of the Minister of the Interior of each different state. These offices impose fines according to a tariff applying throughout the country and set out in a catalogue which can be bought in any bookshop. Thus a motorist would be fined on a scale of penalty which increases with the speed. A further extension of the German scheme means that offences also carry a 'points' score and when a motorist reaches the permitted maximum he faces automatic suspension. A variation on the federal scheme is applied in Bavaria. All the work on the charges is carried out by a police section with a staff of sixty housed in a building in Munich, where Hitler once had his lodgings. But although the Police section can recommend what fine should be imposed the decision rests with three lawyers – 'the three wise men'. The lawyers do not themselves take evidence or question witnesses. This part of

the operation is left to the police section. However, they will listen
to representations on a case before making a decision: while the
motorist also has the option of going to court.

The courts then deal with motorists who either choose not to
have their cases dealt with administratively or are appealing on a
decision. While in addition the most serious of all traffic offences
go automatically to the courts. Drunk-driving would automatically
go to court as too would any kind of traffic offence where injury
resulted. The Germans then have succeeded in grading traffic
offences – and in so doing have averted a breakdown in the courts
system. Before the change it could take a year for a traffic offence
to reach court in Bavaria. While in Hamburg the change has
meant that two hundred thousand traffic offences a year which
were previously dealt with by courts are now dealt with administratively under the catalogue system: of which only about thirty
thousand go to appeal. The courts then have benefited and conse-
quently less police time is now spent in court on traffic work. But
has 'de-criminalising' traffic offences led to less respect for the
traffic regulations? According to the police this has not been the
case. In Munich the director of the police section dealing with
traffic offences said:

Traffic offences are certainly regarded as less criminal. But this
has not led to the public becoming more careless as drivers.
There has been an increase in traffic offences while the scheme
has been in operation but the evidence does not suggest that it
is because of the scheme. The increase has been no more than
average.

Nor is West Germany an exception within Europe. In Italy the
result of legal reforms in 1967 and 1975 is that the majority of
traffic offences are dealt with administratively by fines while the
more serious cases go to court. In France minor offences are dealt
with by tickets which have to be paid within fifteen days. If the
ticket is not paid in the time limit the fine is increased and if this
fine is not paid within fifteen days then the charge is dealt with
by a court. Thus a driver who initially faces a fine of fifty francs
will face an automatic fine of seventy francs if he does not pay and
a maximum fine of eighty francs if he goes to court. In Holland
there are on the spot fines for the least serious offences while for
more serious cases – like speeding – the public prosecutor will

offer the motorist the opportunity of avoiding criminal proceedings by paying a fine. The fines themselves are standardized and a speeding motorist for example, would be fined a set charge per excess kilometre.

The New York Traffic Court

A further example of the same approach comes from outside Europe. New York traffic law was reformed as long ago as 1934 when a distinction was made between criminal motoring offences (like drunken driving, dangerous driving which causes death or injury, driving while under suspension and leaving the scene of an accident) and what were termed 'traffic infractions' which covered the less serious driving offences (like speeding, signal violation, improper lane change and failure to yield the right of way). According to the amending law: 'A traffic infraction is not a crime and the punishment imposed therefore shall not be deemed for any purpose a penal or criminal punishment.' Paradoxically, however, New York – like most other American states – still allowed these non-criminal cases to be dealt with by the criminal courts. By 1969 the criminal courts of the city of New York were handling over eight hundred thousand moving traffic infractions and a further three million two hundred thousand non-moving infractions. The net effect was the imminent break down of the court system and enormous delays in the legal process.

In 1970 the state legislature passed a new law which – following the logic of the position established in 1934 – at last moved traffic infractions out of the criminal legal process. The changes meant that parking offences were dealt with administratively. Offences involving parked vehicles went to the Parking Violation Bureau while, most interestingly of all, the moving infractions were put in the hands of the Administrative Adjudication Bureau (AAB). The position now is that in cases where the AAB has jurisdiction the motorist has three choices. If he pleads 'guilty' then he is able to post his plea together with the prescribed fine to the bureau's central office or pay it in person at one of the various local offices. His second option is to plead 'guilty with an explanation'. This requires an appearance in person by the motorist but not by the policeman and the hearing officer decides. While the last option is of course a plea of 'not guilty' where both the motorist and the policeman appear before the hearing officer and the motorist either

166

personally or through his lawyer has the right to cross examine: while for the police benefit 'not guilty' pleas involving an individual officer are grouped together so that he does not spend unnecessary time waiting to give evidence.

The hearing officers or referees are themselves experienced lawyers but the hearings are much more informal than in the criminal courts and there is an apparently significant difference in the quantum of proof required. In a criminal case guilt must be established 'beyond reasonable doubt': in a case before the traffic court what is required is 'clear and convincing evidence'. However, according to the hearing officers this difference is more apparent than real. One of them said: 'If you want to know the truth it's all a lot of baloney. The judge gets the feeling whether a man is guilty or not.'

It would be too much to claim that that feeling was shared by all the motorists who appear before the traffic courts. But appeal is possible to a three man appeals board and at last resort judicial review both on the decision reached and the sanction imposed. However, judicial review is very rare and indeed few motorists – about four thousand a year – even go to the administrative appeals board. Even by the critical standards of the American Automobile Club the system is seen as fair and for the New York authorities the change has led to a whole list of benefits. Criminal court congestion has been reduced and in New York City alone five courtrooms have been freed from traffic work. A hearing now takes between forty-five and sixty days to process compared with the previous delays of up to a year or more: while police time spent in court has been reduced by half.[7]

So both German and American experience suggest it is possible to distinguish between the seriousness of different motoring offences to the benefit of the courts, police and public. In Britain, however, strangely little official attention has been given to the questions involved – possibly because policy for the motorist falls often awkwardly between two government departments, the Home Office and the Department of Transport. Away from Whitehall the possibility of reforming the traffic laws has received more serious attention. One of the most notable contributions came from two legal academics – Professor D. W. Elliott and Professor Harry Street – in 1968.[8] Their case was that traffic offences fell naturally into two classes: the serious ones which exhibit what a layman would regard as criminality and the less serious ones which are not regarded as criminal. They commented:

> The present law does not recognise this distinction. It insists on treating every transgression, whether offensively anti-social like dangerous driving, or mere breaches of official tidiness like overstaying one's time in a parking bay in exactly the same way as, say, shoplifting or razor slashing – they are investigated by the police and followed by criminal trial and punishment. Here the law is quite out of touch with public opinion, which will never be persuaded of the essential sameness of all breaches of legal rules.

Elliott and Street advocated a division between the two into the less serious traffic breaches – which could be dealt with administratively by ticket – and traffic offences which would be dealt under the present criminal procedure. They went on to propose the establishment of traffic courts and (albeit cautiously) suggested that the criminal procedure with all its safeguards for the accused need not necessarily be required for traffic breaches.

Eight years later in 1976 Sir Robert Mark took up the same theme. Emphasizing that his proposals were 'no more than suggestions for research and consideration' Mark supported a distinction being made.[9] He said:

> Those offences which the public generally believe to involve criminal culpability such as reckless, careless, dangerous or drunken driving should remain within the criminal law with its accepted safeguards for the accused and the stigma of conviction for a criminal offence in the event of a successful prosecution.

On the other hand he believed that:

> A wide variety of other offences not involving culpability – for example parking, speeding not involving danger, offences under the construction and use of motor vehicles could be dealt with by imposition of a penalty under the civil law. No offence involving the possibility of imprisonment could be included in this category. The liberty of the subject not being involved the burden of proof could be reversed.

Mark, however, was less sanguine about new 'ticket' offences. In 1975 more than two million fixed penalty notices were issued – of which only half were paid. The logic of that position drove Mark on to advocate 'on-the-spot fines' where money is paid over directly to the policeman – a proposal that not all policemen would accept.

Nevertheless despite the differences of detail the general approach of Elliott and Street and that of Mark are broadly similar. For the British police the advantage of change along such lines would be that the law itself would be more in line with what the public themselves feel to be right. Viewed from the police stand-point there can be no advantage in seeking to enforce a law which for good reason is regarded as too heavy handed and indiscriminate. 'De-criminalising' the lesser traffic offences will not by itself remove the friction between police and motoring public. Motorists will still protest when they are stopped but it would at least place the law on a more rational basis. By allowing cases to be dealt with administratively or by traffic court the time of the criminal courts and that of the police can be saved. Nor is there any evidence that re-classifying the lesser traffic offences leads to any appreciable increase in those offences. It does, however, serve notice on the motoring public that there remain offences which by any measure are criminal; which cannot be dismissed as 'technical'; and which will lead to severe penalties.

A Traffic Corps?

There are those who would go one stage further and set up a separate traffic corps to police the roads. Proposals vary but the most general proposition is that policing traffic is a separate specialist function which does not require the skills or qualifications of a trained policeman. Often the assumption is made that separately recruited traffic corps exist widely overseas. In Europe this is certainly not the case. All forces have separate traffic sections but in the main the men who work in them come from the ranks of the regular police. Thus in France the men of the CCU (*Compagnie de Circulation Urbaine*) who work in the cities are regular policemen and the motor-cycle patrols on the motorways and major roads come from the CRS. In Germany and Italy traffic officers come from the normal bloodstream of the police service. While in Britain successive Home Secretaries have set their face against anyone but policemen dealing with *moving* traffic offences.

Conventional police wisdom is that it is impossible to separate traffic work from other police work: the motorist stopped on a motorway for a traffic offence may be wanted for armed robbery.

The theory therefore is that police work at this point is indivisible and no advantage would come from creating separate forces under separate command. Perhaps an even stronger reason for retaining the present arrangements is that the assumption made that traffic work is less difficult than other police work is patently not the case. As we have seen it is a major source of possible friction and police forces have sought to take tactical measures to avoid this. Thus in Britain before the last war a 'courtesy cop' scheme was introduced in which the police warned and advised motorists rather than prosecuted them. While today in Germany much of the police-man's psychological training is directed at teaching the policeman how to approach the motorist. Some would still advocate a change to a separate corps on the grounds that public hostility would then centre upon it rather than on the police. Yet it is not at all certain that the public would make such a distinction. What seems far more likely is that the standards of the traffic corps would be below those of the police; that the corps would be heartily disliked by the public; and that the morale (and thus the performance) of such a corps would be low. A more hopeful approach would be to expand the work of traffic wardens in cities and towns. In many European cities wardens are now used to supervise parking meters and experience in London shows that they can also relieve the police on traffic direction, and could if the law was slightly changed help in such jobs as the regulation of bus lanes, which is now the job of the police. Rather than a traffic corps the aim should be an auxiliary force to relieve the police of some of their routine jobs in urban centres.

If then governments decide that moving traffic – both the car and lorry – should basically remain the responsibility of the police they must also face up to one other problem. Each new law which they pass adds to the police task. In some cases – like the seat belt law applied in some but not all European countries – there are added difficulties of enforcing the law which has been passed. Given the pressure on the police governments have a responsibility to keep their new law making to a minimum and only to apply the law when they are satisfied that other methods (persuasion, adver-tising, vehicle design) would not suffice. The passing of law is not an easy option – nor should it be forgotten that there is a financial cost in terms of police manpower in seeing a new law enforced. There is no single policy which can conceivably eliminate the possibility of friction between the motorist and the police. There are, however, sensible steps which any government can take to help. New duties should not easily be placed on the police. Where law is unquestionably necessary (as with drunken driving) the police must be given adequate power to enforce it. Where laws are on the statute book there should be a common-sense division between those which are dealt with by a court and those which are dealt with administratively.

In Britain sensible reform of the way in which traffic offences are dealt with would probably produce the best results. As long ago as 1968 the committee of ministers of the Council of Europe adopted a resolution to institute a simplified procedure for dealing with minor road traffic offences. Such offences included speeding, failure to observe traffic signs and lighting offences. Under the suggested procedure nations were left with the option of fines on-the-spot or by ticket but left the motorist with the option of either complying or going to court. Such a proposal then seeks both to simplify procedure and also to retain the rights of the motorist who chooses to go to court. It is a proposal which could be adopted in Britain – to the benefit of the police and with the approval of the public.

13

Any Complaints?

No police in Europe is required to take complaints from the public more to heart than the English. Other European forces of course investigate the undoubtedly serious complaint when, for instance, there is an allegation that a policeman has committed a crime. But no one else goes to such infinite pains to record and investigate *every* complaint from the public. The English will even investigate a charge that a policeman has been seen smoking on duty although this often takes some doing. One policeman with a long experience of investigating complaints said: 'You have to see the policeman who was on duty. He may well say he was not smoking so you then have to see if there are any witnesses – like the men on the building site opposite.' A year or two ago there was a case where a policeman who was serving a summons had to knock twice on the door to make himself heard above the blaring television set. In the later complaint the policeman was accused of knocking 'too loudly' and the case was investigated at an estimated cost of £750. The policeman himself resigned in disgust.[1]

Not surprisingly this system is often deeply resented by the policemen themselves. As one senior officer put it: 'The new policeman feels that the scales are weighted against him and that he has come into a profession where anybody can put him in jeopardy by just a phone call or a letter.' The jeopardy is real enough. A policeman who is the subject of a complaint can remain under suspension until the case is settled. The power to suspend rests with the chief constable and although largely confined to the most serious cases inevitably leads to injustice when innocent men are suspended from duty. Traditionally discipline has been the undisputed prerogative of chief constables and inside the service the view has always been that chief constables have been harder on the police offender than any outside body ever would have been. For example, acquittal in a court of law has not prevented chief constables from dismissing the policemen involved. In one case in 1970 three policemen were acquitted after a twenty day trial at the Old Bailey but nevertheless were forced to resign.[2] There is then some truth in the claim that there has been one law for the policeman and another for the public. What has been less obvious is that the stricter law has been applied against policemen.

Another widely held police view is that the system plays into the hands of not only the trivial but also the persistent complainer. Policemen tend to share Burke's view that 'it is a general popular error to imagine that the loudest complainants for the public to be the most anxious for its welfare.' Most police forces can name a number of incorrigible complainants. In one case a man made thirty-four separate complaints secure in the knowledge that he had little to lose. For unlike other bodies who receive complaints from the public – such as the Press Council – the police do not publish the details of both the proven and unproven cases or the names of those who have made them. By and large the complaints that receive publicity are those which lead to prosecutions – although as Table 6 shows this gives a totally misleading impression.

Table 6
COMPLAINTS AGAINST THE POLICE (ENGLAND AND WALES)

	1969	1970	1971	1972	1973	1974	1975	1976	1977
plaints against e Police	11,814	12,044	12,271	15,543	16,155	17,454	19,205	22,738	27,700
s leading to iminal Charges cluding those for affic Offences)*	135	152	90	127	110	105	128	124	
s leading Disciplinary arges†	208	222	209	258	186	189	247	182	

*es not include cases where charges are brought in a subsequent year.
some cases the relevant complaint may have been made in an earlier
r.

In other cases the complaints procedure acts as a final appeal for men convicted in the courts on police evidence. A Commander at Scotland Yard put the point:

These are the men who complain from prison. They have been convicted and they have gone to appeal. In both cases they have lost. Then they must choose a new tack. They complain of the police. By law we must investigate their complaint and it can be expensive. We have to get the transcript of the trial and for a ten day trial this can cost anywhere between £400 and £600. It may tie a detective down for three or four weeks. To my mind these kind of complaints are much more objectionable than the complaint from the old lady in Richmond who has never before heard a policeman swear.

In cold statistics the English position is this. On average less than one complaint in ten holds up after examination: and of these only a minute proportion lead to convictions in a court of law – and even then most convictions are for traffic offences. Yet to achieve these relatively paltry results the police have to sift through over twenty-five thousand complaints a year. No one knows the exact cost of this exercise but what is known is that many senior officers (for the law requires that only senior officers should investigate complaints) are tied down by it. In the Metropolitan Police in London alone around one hundred policemen do nothing else but investigate complaints against other policemen. Scarce police resources are diverted from other, and some would argue, more important tasks. The question must arise whether it is all worth it.

Giving evidence to a committee reviewing the English complaints procedure the Association of Chief Police Officers remarked that the constant pressure for ever more elaborate complaints machinery came from 'a small number of persons with a voice out of proportion to their numbers.'[3] As a statement of fact this is undoubtedly true although pressure groups like the National Council for Civil Liberties are entitled to reply that exactly the same remarks can be made about any group seeking change. Certainly it does not settle the argument. For all recent police history shows that the only time when public attention really turns to the complaints procedure is when the police is under attack. It is then that the small voice can very easily become louder, and, of course, it is then that it is very much in the police interest to be able to satisfy the public that their procedures are adequate to deal with any abuse of police power.

In the past the police have not always been able to do this. In 1957 police standards in Britain were brought into public question after two senior officers in the Brighton force were convicted on charges of corruption and shortly afterwards by another trial in which the Chief Constable of Worcester was convicted of fraud. Attention having been aroused it then proved remarkably difficult to satisfy the public on two further cases which were in no way as serious. The first was the Thurso case in Scotland when it was alleged that two policemen had assaulted a fifteen year old boy outside a cafe. The case was debated in Parliament and it needed the full paraphernalia of a Government Tribunal of Inquiry to establish that one of the policemen, under severe provocation, had indeed struck the boy.[4] The second involved the actor Brian Rix who had been stopped for speeding by a policeman on traffic duty. Another driver, Mr Garrett, who had been just behind Mr Rix, stopped to speak to him and offer evidence which would have contradicted the policeman. Accounts of what then happened vary but what is not in dispute is that the policeman took Mr Garrett to the local station with the intention of charging him with assaulting a policeman. The Station Officer, however, refused to accept the charge and Mr Garrett later issued a writ against the policeman for assault and false imprisonment. In the event the action was settled out of court by the police force concerned making a payment of £300 but this only added fuel to the fire. The suspicion then became that the force was covering up for one of its men. Again the case was raised in the House of Commons and during the debate the Home Secretary, Mr R. A. Butler, promised a wide inquiry to examine relations between police and public – an inquiry which became the Royal Commission on the police.[5]

Another force which was unable to satisfy the public with the way it handled complaints was the Amsterdam police in 1966. Following the riots the police came under fierce fire and allegations were made freely that the Dutch police had used excessive force and carried out indiscriminate arrests. Some of these charges were undoubtedly true but most were exaggerated or false. The difficulty for the police authorities was that they were unable to convince the public that this was the case. Up to 1966 nearly all investigations into complaints against the police were made by the individual forces themselves. Such an arrangement certainly recognized the sovereignty of individual chief constables, but it also played into the hands of committed police critics. For if charges were dismissed then the critics simply retorted that the force had acted as judge and jury in its own cause. It is the most common criticism of any police complaints procedure and it is also the most difficult to answer.

The cases show clearly enough the danger for the police. Amidst the mass of the trivial and the unsubstantiated comes the genuine complaint which suddenly focuses public attention upon the police. Unless the police can show that such complaints are dealt with surely and swiftly they may well be judged by them. Their protests that these are but a small minority will go unheeded. It is therefore very much in the police interest to have a complaints procedure which does not leave them vulnerable to future events. The police cannot afford to be lulled into a sense of security at a time of relative calm and even less by the letters they receive urging them to ignore their critics. For it is an interesting fact that with the increase in urban guerrilla activities and of violence generally many of the letters that the police now receive urge them to take more repressive action. In Bonn, for example, eighty per cent of the letters received by the Federal Ministry of the Interior now urge that the police should take a tougher line in demonstrations. An example came in April 1973 when the President of South Vietnam visited the German capital. Demonstrators occupied the City Hall in protest and eventually were ejected by the police. Some of the demonstrators complained of police brutality but the overwhelming public reaction, as measured by the letters received at the Ministry, was that the police should have gone in sooner and dealt with the demonstration more thoroughly. Yet as every politician knows, and every policeman should know, public moods change quickly. Those who urge tougher action today will complain of brutality tomorrow.

The only sensible policy for the police to pursue is to show that they will always deal fairly with any complaint and that certain action will be taken against any police offenders. Even the apparently trivial must be investigated. What is trivial to the police may be a matter of concern for the individual, and in any event the initial complaint may not always reveal the true charge. One policeman said:

A complaint that looks serious may turn out to be trivial. On the face of it the complaint may look very serious indeed but it turns out that it is all concerned with the police having towed away the man's car. On the other hand an apparently trivial complaint can sometimes be much more serious. There was one case where what looked like a minor case turned out to be a case of a policeman committing burglary.

Yet the most elaborate complaints system in the world will be worth very little unless the police can demonstrate its impartiality. The ideal – as a thousand editorials have urged – is a system which is not only fair but seen to be fair. But translating this generalization into practice has not proved easy.

In the last fifteen years three inquiries in England have examined this question. In 1962 the Royal Commission on the police proposed changes which were later put into effect by the 1964 Police Act. In 1969 a working party was set up by the Home Secretary which reported in 1971; and in 1973 a further Home Office working party was established which reported in 1974. By the end the search was quite simply for 'an independent element' in the complaints procedure which would establish its impartiality to the public preferably without antagonizing the police. There were two distinct views on the form of this independent element. The first was that there should be an independent tribunal which would only be brought into action after the police had been given the chance to clear up the complaint themselves. The second view was that there was not much point in establishing an independent check if there had been no similar check on the investigation itself. We have then to be quite certain what we mean by 'independent'.

Most policemen would oppose bitterly any plan for a body of independent investigators formed separate from the police and here their case is undoubtedly strong. One policeman said:

> The practical difficulties are overwhelming. The investigation of a complaint involves exactly the same techniques as any other criminal investigation. It needs the same background – the same knowledge of where to go for help.

Another policeman in London said:

> At the end of the investigation the policeman has the duty to recommend what action should be taken as the result of his report. To do this he must know the kind of pressure that officers work under. He must know what it's like to be at Brixton station between 10.00 and 12.00 on a Saturday night. The police would not have confidence in investigators who did not have that kind of experience. They would be regarded as just theorists.

Perhaps the overwhelming argument against a separate body to investigate the police is the legal one. The police operate under the law and it would be a curious anomaly if they were to be made subject to a different form of legal procedure. However, the difficulty remains of demonstrating to the public that an investigation of policemen is independent if it is carried out by the police.

The solution which has been adopted in Europe is to show that the investigating police have no operational connection with the policemen under investigation. Thus the only loyalty involved will be the general one that they are all policemen. Probably Holland has gone furthest in seeking to establish the independence of the police investigators. The result of 1966 was that the small state detective force was given the task of investigating the most serious complaints against the police. The force comes under the command of the district prosecutors and ultimately the Ministry of Justice and the men who serve in it are recruited from the police but never return to their old force. They spend the rest of their careers in the better paid although less popular state force – 'they are feared as well as respected' said one Dutch policeman – investigating other policemen and carrying out other delicate assignments like the investigation of state officials suspected of corruption. The decision on which cases go to the state force and which are dealt with locally is taken by the district prosecutor but a complaint arising from a serious demonstration will automatically go to the special force. Their report then goes back to the prosecutor who will decide if a prosecution should take place. If the decision is taken against prosecution then the complainant can appeal to the district court who will decide if a prosecution should be attempted – although it will not decide on guilt or innocence.

The same principle is followed in France and in Germany. In Paris a complaint against the police will be investigated by the department in charge of discipline. The department is staffed by senior policemen who are members of the *police judiciaire* who operate independently of the rest of the force. It is not a popular posting and as one readily conceded: 'Most of the men do not want to come to this office. They do not like checking on their colleagues and they realise only too well that they are not liked and viewed with fear.' Similarly in Bavaria serious complaints are handled by a special section reporting directly to the President of Police. In England various methods have been used to establish the independence of the investigating police and in extreme cases the Home Secretary can order an investigation to be carried out by a member from another force. But it was not until 1972 – long after the principle had been adopted in the rest of Europe – that a real effort was to be made to underline this independence.

The complaints branch at Scotland Yard – the A10 branch – was a radical departure. Since 1879 investigations into complaints against the Metropolitan Police had been under the control of the Assistant Commissioner with responsibility for investigating crime – although it was the Deputy Commissioner who was in charge of discipline in the force. When policemen from outside London were called in to investigate the most serious charges they were not given executive power but acted as advisers to the investigation which remained under the ultimate control of the Assistant Commissioner. Even when one of the Inspectors of Constabulary was asked to examine charges made against members of the Flying Squad in 1970 by *The Times* he did no more than act as a consultant to the investigation The defect in this arrangement was the constitutional one: it appeared that there was a question of double loyalty. Many of the most serious charges obviously involved members of the CID. However, the Assistant Commissioner who was in the final event responsible for the standards of the department was also directly responsible for investigating those standards. When the complaints branch was formed this position was changed. The branch now answered directly to the Deputy Commissioner in charge of discipline and the Assistant Commissioner in charge of crime was by-passed. This position continues today (although the branch has now been renamed CIB2) and investigates the most serious complaints made against the Metropolitan Police. In practice this means that they investigate about ten per cent of the complaints made while the remainder are dealt with at divisional level.

The independence of this investigating unit is underlined by its very structure. All the one hundred men in the unit are experienced policemen: almost a third are of the rank of detective superintendent or above and all have a minimum of six years service. They stay with the branch for two or three years and during that time do nothing else but investigate complaints. No one pretends it is a popular job. One senior officer at Scotland Yard said:

The men employed in the branch are chosen. I don't think many would volunteer. They are in fact some of the best people we have. Many will go on to promotion. It is a good way of seeing what goes wrong with the police. But I don't think many would want to stay here for much longer than two or three years. There simply is not the same job satisfaction.

Scotland Yard have in effect produced a variation on the Dutch scheme. Rather than forming a permanent body of 'untouchables' the men in the complaints branch come on secondment and then return to the main blood stream of the force. Many policemen would feel that this was a healthier arrangement.

So by the time the 1973 Home Office working party came to take evidence the Metropolitan Police had already taken a giant step towards ensuring and demonstrating the fairness of their investigation system. Nevertheless Robert Mark still advocated one further step. The case he put forward was that the results of the police inquiry should be available for examination and comment by a non-police body: thus demolishing the claim that the police were judge and jury in their own cause. His proposal was for a complaints review authority (ideally the Parliamentary Commissioner assisted by assessors) who could examine any complaint at the request of a member of the public or policemen *after* the internal police investigation and disciplinary procedure had been completed. Although the review authority would have no power to initiate criminal or disciplinary proceedings it would have a persuasive effect in that chief constables would know that their decision could be checked and costs could be awarded to the complainant. The Mark scheme was therefore simple and built on top of the A10 Branch – which had been sufficiently accepted by the public that only some thirty complainants a year were expressing dissatisfaction with the way that their complaints had been handled.

But Mark's view did not prevail. Instead the then Home Secretary, Roy Jenkins, produced a scheme which was both complex and widely attacked by some of the strongest supporters of change. Nevertheless – after protracted debate – the proposals became law in June 1977. The essence of the scheme is that a new Complaints Board has been set up composed of non-policemen. Each complaint is still investigated by the police and if a criminal offence is alleged the case will go for decision to the Director of Public Prosecutions. The Board cannot question the decision of the Director on criminal proceedings nor can the Board vary disciplinary charges brought by the Deputy Chief Constable responsible for ensuring that complaints are investigated. However, the Board can direct that the charges are heard by a disciplinary tribunal rather than, as is the normal practice, the Chief Constable sitting alone. If a tribunal is appointed this will consist of the Chief Constable and two members of the Board. In that situation the Chief Constable can be outvoted on the question of guilt or innocence. When the Deputy Chief Constable decides *not* to prefer a disciplinary charge he must automatically send the papers to the Board. It is then open to the Board to recommend and in the last resort direct that charges should be brought – charges brought on the direction of the Board will automatically be heard by a disciplinary tribunal.

In addition the Home Office have sought to write in safeguards for the policeman. Thus a policeman who has been charged with and acquitted of a criminal offence cannot be then charged under the disciplinary code if the offence is 'in substance the same.' However, when a case involves both a criminal offence and misconduct not amounting to a crime the two can be separated and even if he is acquitted of criminal charges the policeman can still face disciplinary proceedings. A further regulation allows Police Federation funds to be used to pursue actions for slander or libel where for example, the complainant seeks to cast doubt upon a policeman's 'fitness to be a member of police force.' While another regulation enables the investigating officer to recommend that the 'complaint is trivial or ill-founded or that the effort involved in pursuing it would be disproportionate' – the hope being that the effort spent on the undoubtedly trivial will be reduced.

No one then can seriously doubt that England has the most elaborate complaints procedure in Europe. Whether it will turn out to be most effective is more open to doubt. Although the investigating system at Scotland Yard has proved itself as both an effective check and as a means of satisfying the public there has been no move to make it standard. The method of investigation is left to individual forces. In contrast, however, the disciplinary authority of the individual chief constable over his force has been diminished. Ultimate decisions on discipline now rest with a three man tribunal in which the chief constable can be outvoted. Under the old system a policeman would be required to resign or advised to resign. The fear of some chief constables today is that the dishonest policeman could now take his case to the disciplinary tribunal and remain in the service.

The risk (and irony) is that the Home Office in their determination to make the complaints procedure appear fair may have made it more difficult for chief constables to protect the real public interest. It is of course too early to say whether these fears will be proved right, but what seems certain is that even the new legislation has not stilled the argument. Those who want radical change see the new law as a first step: most policemen see the change as an unnecessary and expensive piece of additional bureaucracy. The risk is that the new system will end up pleasing neither police nor public.

14

The Next Ten Years

Over the last ten years Europe and its police forces have been subjected to one new challenge after another. In the late Sixties riots in the streets almost brought down one of Europe's most powerful governments and seriously troubled all the others. The cataclysm was avoided but by the late Seventies a brand of demonstrator had emerged who was prepared to stop at nothing – including murder – in his efforts to force change or bring down governments. In the late Sixties the threat of the terrorist was taken seriously in Ulster but hardly contemplated elsewhere in Europe. By the late Seventies there was scarcely a country in the Common Market which had not faced a major terrorist attack. Bombings, kidnappings, sieges had become everyday events: they still caused concern but no longer surprise. While throughout the ten years the relentless rise in crimes of violence provided the most disturbing trend in the criminal statistics. The containment of violence had never seemed more important.

Only a hopeless optimist would expect the next ten years to be any less eventful. New demands are likely to be made of the police and some policemen already see problem areas which they believe could develop easily into crisis areas. The most fundamental of these is the situation produced by the entry into West Europe of several million foreign workers and immigrants. For the police the effect of the influx is that they find themselves dealing with a new public who not only have their own different customs but also their own attitudes and views. Easy assumptions that the new-comers and their children will automatically come to share the general national view of the police are not borne out by experience. Britain illustrates the point. Immigration for settlement in Britain from the West Indies, India and Pakistan started seriously in the 1950s.

It continued uncontrolled up to 1962 and throughout the rest of the 1960s the major immigration was by wives and children coming to join the head of the family. The result is that today the young coloured population in Britain is made up predominantly of men and women who were brought in as children or who were born in the country. Their attitude to the police, however, contrasts sharply with the general view.

As we have seen the police are probably the most respected professional group in Britain among the general public. A survey carried out for *The Times* among young immigrants aged between sixteen and twenty-four showed a very different picture.[1] As Table 7 shows nearly two out of three young West Indians believed that the police dealt unfairly; while forty-three per cent believed that the courts dealt unfairly. Among Indians and Pakistanis the figures are better – but still worse than the general view. Confirmation of this picture came in 1972 from evidence given to the House of Commons Select Committee on Race Relations and Immigration. Again it was the West Indian community who were most outspoken. According to one West Indian organization: '. . . to state that a sizeable proportion of the West Indian community no longer trust the police is to confer a euphemism upon a situation which for many has reached a level equal to fear.' The Jamaican High Commission reported signs of increasing tension 'as fear, mistrust and misunderstanding on both sides have resulted in polarization of attitudes'; and the West Indian Deputy Chairman of the Community Relations Commission said that 'the real conflict is between the police and the West Indian' – particularly the young West Indian. In London a community relations officer added that young black people saw the police as alarming representatives of a society which treated them badly.[2]

Table 7
ATTITUDES TO POLICE

	INDIANS %	WEST INDIANS %	PAKISTANIS %
Police deal fairly	66	23	75
Police deal unfairly	31	64	23
No information	3	13	2
Courts deal fairly	73	46	83
Courts deal unfairly	23	43	9
No information	4	11	8

Among European policemen there is a tendency to talk to British visitors about *'your'* problem of immigration. It is a strange view – given that the Common Market is sometimes said not to have nine members but ten. The tenth is half jestingly claimed to be the vast number of foreign workers who now live in the different countries of the EEC. In West Germany alone there are over two million 'guest workers' drawn mainly from Turkey, Yugoslavia, Greece, Spain and Italy. France has over one and a half million mainly from Portugal, Spain, Algeria and Italy. While Belgium, the Netherlands and Luxembourg all have substantial numbers. In addition there is an unknown army of illegal entrants often brought in by firms anxious to make use of hard-working, compliant and cheap labour. In theory, the foreign workers' system is different to the assured permanent settlement offered to immigrant families in Britain. Although many foreign workers have come to Europe, saved money and returned home, many others have brought their families and stayed. A second generation is growing up who are not likely to accept the often squalid living conditions and limited horizons of their parents.

As in Britain there is every sign that new difficulties are being stored up for the police. Often the newcomers provoke resentment among the established communities where they settle. In 1972 there were riots in Rotterdam which stemmed from a shortage of low cost housing in the city and the fear of local people that they were being crowded out by the foreign workers. The following year in Marseilles there was a further example of the tension just beneath the surface when an Algerian immigrant worker stabbed a bus driver and provoked a series of reprisal killings in which seven Algerians were murdered. In other cases the immigrant group has little interest in integrating into the host communities and regard the police – the most obvious representative of the community – with hostility. An extreme example here is the small Moluccan community in Holland who were ousted from Indonesia but who retain a hopeless ambition to return. Already the frustration among the young Moluccans has spilt over into terrorist actions and few see anything other than continuing difficulties. As one policeman said: 'They don't want to assimilate into the population for they are waiting to return. The young people don't get a good education and therefore they don't get good jobs. It is a vicious circle.'

In the end, however, the more serious problems are likely to be caused by the foreign workers, and families who want (or at any rate choose) to stay to take advantage of the high standard of living inside the European community. The scope for misunderstanding between the new settlers and the receiving community is enormous. As an official of the Foreign Workers Foundation in Rotterdam put it:

> Misunderstanding can result from language, from different expectations or simply from tradition. The Turkish foreign worker sees the official operating in Holland through the eyes of someone brought up in Turkey. The same is true of the police. The Turkish foreign worker tends to fear the police. They remember them as a strong authoritarian body. They see them as an enemy.

Among the first acquiescent generation such attitudes probably will not cause too many open conflicts. The difficulty comes with the succeeding generations when fear and suspicion can easily become aggressive hostility.

Of course it is true that it is not the police who shoulder the major responsibility for coping with the entry and settlement of foreign workers and immigrants into Europe. If governments do not succeed in providing better housing then a major source of discontent (and in police terms trouble) will continue leaving particularly the young a prey to extreme political groups who already see the immigrants as hopeful recruiting material. The police, however, often carry the can for more fundamental complaints. *The Times* survey which showed almost two-thirds of the young West Indian population believing the police dealt unfairly also showed one other important fact – seventy-three per cent of the West Indians interviewed had never had any personal encounters with the police. In the case of the Pakistanis the figure was seventy-seven per cent and Indians eighty-three per cent. Their view of the police then partly represented their general view of the country in which they were seeking their future and the extent to which their aspirations were being realized – as well as reflecting general assumptions made about the police in their communities. For the policeman findings of this kind must appear to amply describe a battle he can never expect to win and certainly it is true that he cannot win it alone. Yet given a realistic general policy-making response from governments the police task is far from hopeless.

In Britain a range of actions has been taken by the police. Com-

munity relations officers who have responsibility for liaison between the police and immigrant communities have been appointed
in all forces where a problem exists and attention has been given
to appointing the right men for this often difficult job. As the
Commons Select Committee proposed:

> Chief officers of police should realize the importance of appoint-
> ing the right person to be a community liaison officer and then
> of making sure that the post is not allowed to become a dead
> end. Women have a special contribution to make in such ap-
> pointments . . . All senior police community liaison officers
> should have access to senior officers, including chief officers of
> police, when they want it.

Police pay visits to schools with the aim of explaining the police
role; while race relations is now part of the policeman's own training syllabus. Undoubtedly more could be achieved if forces were
up to realistic strength (once more it is the city forces who face the
major problems) so allowing more men to be deployed; and if
police training in Britain was longer. Nevertheless a very substantial start has been made and both police and Home Office have
recognized that in this area also it is not enough for the policeman
to say 'my uniform is my authority.' As Robert Carr, then Home
Secretary, put it in October 1973:

> It is not enough – and no doubt never was – for the police merely
> to know and enforce the law. They need an adequate under-
> standing of the aspirations of the different sections of the com-
> munity in which they move if they are to establish the mutual
> trust on which successful policing depends.

Given that Britain was first in Europe to experience massive
settlement of workers from outside the national boundaries it is not
surprising that the British police should have taken the earliest
action to try and cope with some of the problems caused. Elsewhere in Europe very little is being done by police forces. Yet it is
probable that over the next decade some European forces will be
facing similar problems to the British police. It is surely here that
there is a point of general application.

The police in Europe today face many of the same problems:
crime, terrorism, traffic, relations with young people and minorities.
Nevertheless all too often forces seek to develop their own policies
without any regard to experience elsewhere. The French police

know no more about the British police attempt to improve race relations than the British in the Sixties knew about regional crime squads in France. Several European forces are tentatively experimenting with women police when Britain has had them for years. For years the German and Dutch police had a pay structure which was streets ahead of the British model. The truth is that every nation would benefit from a wider exchange of information. It is here that there is an undoubted opportunity for Europe.

The differences in national legal systems was recognized by the authors of the Treaty of Rome. There is no requirement that Europe should harmonise its criminal code: and no demand for a European force – which in any event would be difficult to form given the differences in legal procedure. Operational co-operation between forces will certainly increase over the next ten years but the aim should be not the development of new forms of organization (a course much beloved by policemen and Common Market enthusiasts alike) but ways in which the experience of policemen themselves can be widened. Here an institute of police studies would be of immense help. Such an institute could bring together policemen – middle ranks as well as leaders – from all nine members of the Common Market so that practical experience could be shared. While such an institute could also initiate studies of questions causing concern or likely to develop. It would be one further step to recognizing the police as an unquestionably professional body with the need for as deep a professional training as possible.

There is one point which is certain about the next ten years and that is that the police job will become more demanding and more complex – and even more important. Governments must certainly demonstrate to the public that there will be effective checks on abuse of power and that forces are subject to the public they serve, through accountability to elected assemblies and to the law. But governments must also demonstrate to the police that they regard them as a professional group – to be well trained and well paid in line with the responsibilities they carry. A central task for the governments of the European Community over the next decade is to improve the lot of the policeman himself. No nation should take that more to heart than Britain.

References

1 The Police Idea

1 Leon Radzinowicz, *History of English Criminal Law,* Vols 2 and 3, Stevens, 1956
2 T. A. Critchley, *A History of Police in England and Wales, 900 – 1966,* Constable, 1976
3 Select Committee to inquire into burglaries and robberies in the Cities of London and Westminster, 1770
4 Debate on Gordon Riots, *Parliamentary History of England* Vol 21, 1780–81
5 Debates on London and Westminster Police Bill, *Parliamentary History of England* Vol 25, 1785–86
6 P. J. Stead, *The Police of Paris,* Staples, 1957
7 T. A. Critchley and P. D. James, *The Maul and the Pear Tree –* for examination of case, including doubts about identity of murderer, Constable, 1971
8 Parliamentary Debates 2nd Series, Vol 21, 1829
9 First Report of the Commissioners appointed to inquire as to the best means of establishing an efficient Constabulary Force in the Counties of England and Wales, 1839
10 Select Committee appointed to consider the expediency of adopting a more uniform system of policing in England, Wales and Scotland, 1853

2 The Making of a Police State

1 Robert M. W. Kempner, *Research Studies of the State College of Washington* Vol XIII, June 1945
2 *ibid.*
3 Albert Grzesinski, *Inside Germany,* New York, 1939
4 B. Gisevius, *To the Bitter End,* Jonathan Cape, 1948
5 Edward Crankshaw, *Gestapo,* Putnam, 1956

3 The Tactics of Provocation

1 *Sunday Times,* 19 June 1966
2 *The Times,* 10 June 1966
3 *The Guardian,* 18 June 1966
4 Cohn Bendit, *Obsolete Communism,* Deutsch, 1968
5 Christian Fouchet, *Memoires d'Hier et de Demain,* Plon, 1971
6 Patrick Seale and Maureen McConville, *French Revolution 1968,* Penguin, 1968
7 John Gretton, *Students and Workers,* Macdonald, 1969

4 Europe Today

1 *The Economist,* 23 March 1968
2 Tariq Ali, *The Coming British Revolution,* Jonathan Cape, 1972
3 An account of this demonstration is given by Dr Maurice Punch in *Police,* February 1976
4 Mary McCarthy on 'The Demo', *Sunday Times Magazine,* 8 December 1968
5 Royal Commission on the Police, 1962, Cmnd 1728
6 Opinion Research Centre, *Sunday Times,* 21 December 1969
7 Opinion Research Centre, *Sunday Times,* 26 November 1973
8 Wickert Institute, 1968
9 Published 25 September 1973

5 The Big, The Small and The National

There are very few books dealing with the organization of different national police forces but see *The World's Police* by James Cramer (Cassell, 1964). For the arguments on the organization of the British police see particularly The Royal Commission on the Police, 1962

6 Officers and Men

1 *Recruitment of Police with Higher Educational Qualifications into the Police Service,* Home Office Report, 1967, Chairman: Dick Taverne. HMSO
2 Parliamentary Questions, *Hansard,* 15 July 1976 and 30 November 1977
3 Home Office Circular No 94/1973 and Appendices.

7 The Policemen

1 Interim Report of Royal Commission on the Police, Cmnd 1222 HMSO, 1960
2 Earl of Desborough, Report on Police Pay, 1919

8 The Terrorist

1 Report of the Commissioner of Police for the Metropolis for 1973, HMSO, June 1974
2 *Violence and Civil Disturbances in Northern Ireland in 1969,* Report of Tribunal of Inquiry, HMSO, April 1972
3 *The Guardian,* 1 May 1974
4 Speech by Sir Robert Mark at Leicester University, March 1976
5 Robert Moss, *Counter Terrorism,* Economist Brief, 1972

9 Crime and the Law

1 Sir Leon Radzinowicz, *Them and Us,* a lecture given in London, 1972

2 Sir Robert Mark, *Social Violence,* a lecture, 19 August 1971
3 *Sunday Times,* 26 May 1974
4 *The German Code of Criminal Procedure,* introduction by Dr Eberhard Schmidt, Sweet & Maxwell, 1965
5 *The Times,* 1 June 1977
6 A. V. Sheehan, *Criminal Procedure in Scotland and France,* HMSO, 1975
7 Letter to *The Times,* 25 September, 1975
8 Sir Robert Mark, *A Matter of Conviction,* Criminal Law Review, June 1966
9 Criminal Law Revision Committee, Eleventh Report, HMSO, 1972

10 Full Circle?

1 *The Listener,* March 1971
2 *The Times* Law Report, 29 July 1974
3 *The Times,* 18 April 1974
4 Report to the Home Secretary from the Commissioner of Police of the Metropolis on the Actions of Police Officers concerned with the case of Kenneth Joseph Lennon, 31 July 1974. HC 351. HMSO

11 Police and Morals

1 The Obscene Publications Act 1969
2 *The Daily Telegraph,* 5 October 1973
3 Affidavit of the Commissioner of Police. R v. The Commissioner of the Metropolitan Police, ex parte Blackburn, October 1972
4 Quoted in R v. Commissioner of the Metropolitan Police, ex parte Blackburn, IAER 1968
5 Kursaal Casino Ltd v. Crickett (1) 1966, 1 WLR
  Kursaal Casino Ltd v. Crickett (2) 1967, 1 WLR
6 R v. Commissioner of the Metropolitan Police, 1968

12 Traffic and the Law

1 Report on Police Pay, 1932
2 Royal Commission on the Police, 1962
3 Transport Policy, Consultation Document, 1976. HMSO
4 *Drinking and Driving,* a report by a committee, Chairman Frank Blennerhassett, 1976. HMSO
5 Road Traffic Act 1972, Section 8
6 Blennerhassett Report
7 A full description is set out in *An Exemplary Project* New York State Department of Motor Vehicles, Administrative Adjudication Bureau, US Government Printing Office
8 Professor D. W. Elliott and Professor Harry Street, *Road Accidents,* Penguin, 1968
9 Sir Robert Mark, a speech to the Motor Agents Association, 1976

13 Any Complaints?

1 *The Daily Telegraph,* 4 October 1973
2 *The Spectator,* 3 April 1971
3 *The Handling of Complaints Against the Police,* Cmnd 5582, HMSO, March 1974
4 *The Allegation of Assault on John Walters,* Cmnd 718, HMSO, April 1959
5 *Hansard,* 18 November 1959

14 The Next Ten Years

1 *The Times,* February 1971
2 Select Committee on Race Relations and Immigration, HMSO, August 1972

Index

193